AF325834

You Can't Be Serious When You're 60

Madeleine Melquiond

You Can't Be Serious When You're 60

Max Milo
ESSAIS-DOCUMENTS

© Max Milo Éditions

Collection Essais-Documents, Paris, 2023

www.maxmilo.com

ISBN : 978-2-315-01261-9

to Clémence Borin

Foreword

The age of life between 60 and 70 is paradoxical in modern Western societies. Class cleavages persist despite the dominant discourse, marked by the cliché that people in their sixties are all rich, handsome and fit. In reality, we came of age at the end of the prosperous post-war years, known as the "Trente Glorieuses", and while we didn't experience the end of the welfare state, we did experience its first signs of decay. Our pensions reproduce the same disparities as those affecting society as a whole.

This very cliché is contradictory. Alongside the assertion that we're a privileged generation in every sense of the word (health, beauty, wealth), we're judged as retarded in a wheezy idealism and already diminished by physical and cerebral deficiencies that we'd seek to grotesquely mask.

To these clichés, "advisors" of all stripes (who help to create and feed them) propose miracle remedies, a ready-made, supposed to protect us from ridicule, keep us in a state of static youth, and make us live "to the full" and "enjoy" our sixties. On the one hand, precautions to take to avoid deteriorating; on the other, "activities" to "intensely" live this "new stage" of life through the dual means of entertainment and altruism, this aspect playing on our presumed guilt as rebellious, spoiled and irresponsible children of '68. These coaches, to give them a fashionable term, also prepare us for later life, by inviting us to examine our conscience, or even to undergo a spiritual conversion. I've entitled this section "Do this, don't do that".

My experience of mid-life is somewhat different from the clichés —which I illustrate to my own detriment— and I'm resistant to the advice of our mentors —to which I sometimes grumble. In my circle of friends and acquaintances, I find that many of them put up with these preconceived ideas and loud injunctions, not without astonishment but not without a sense of humor.

It's probably not a bad idea to play a different kind of music.

THE CLICHES

CHAPTER I
YOUNG, RICH AND FIT!

1945: end of the war. The birth rate takes off. The baby boom begins. The pampered children of victory, we pose, perfumed with Cadum soap, for Kodak photos. Progressive social legislation, combined with the need for manpower in a devastated country, paved the way for full employment. Many families enjoyed a comfortable lifestyle, of which household arts were the symbol. This good fortune continued for thirty years, the Trente Glorieuses, although some claim that the expression comes from Gloria milk, the basis of our baby bottles. Thanks to Ovaltine and Phosphatine, we become vigorous children. We enter high school. We're baccalaureate holders. We flock to university. The old walls of the lecture halls, designed for an elite, crack under the thrust of our young minds.

Our parents know the messiness of war and the price of peace. So they're principled people. They tell us that we have to make the most of the opportunity we've been given by being serious and hard-working, and therefore chaste before marriage. Alas, having known nothing of the rigors of the Occupation, we have a carefree, rebellious spirit. In March 1968, when boys were forbidden to sleep in girls' dormitories (and vice versa) at the Cité Universitaire de Nanterre, we launched a revolt. The movement snowballed into May 68. A general fuck. Our youthful effervescence lasts until Grand-père de Gaulle threatens to fire cannons and gathers all our parents at Place de la Concorde with tricolored flags. Our revolution is consigned to the closet of utopias...

During this golden age, we experienced no wars, famines or major disasters (in France, that is). We worked in a buoyant economic context that today ensures comfortable pensions. We're also part of what some sociologists call "gentrification". We haven't bought noble districts, as the word might suggest, but homes that are now worth a fortune. It's a disgrace to see old people gobbling themselves up, while young people are going from one short-term job to the next...

Having had our arms tattooed with BCG and annual lung x-rays, we've also benefited to the full from spectacular advances in medicine and surgery. Gone were smallpox, tuberculosis and other infectious diseases. No more heart attacks. One cancer in two is cured. AIDS, which appeared more recently, has exacted a heavy toll, but sufferers are living longer, thanks to all our donors. The sequencing of the human genome opens up unprecedented prospects. We have good reason to hope that senile dementia (or Alzheimer's disease) will be defeated. Life expectancy climbs to 84.5 years for women and 77.6 years for men. Blowing out 100 candles is becoming commonplace: 17,087 cakes in 2012! Ain't life grand?

To write this golden legend, we had to put aside a few trivial facts. Forgotten were the wars in Korea, Indochina and Algeria, which claimed the lives of many conscripts; vanished was the general strike which, in May and June 68, paralyzed the country

more than the barricades on Boulevard Saint-Michel; oblite-
rated, the oil crisis of 1974, the starting point for restructuring,
relocations and other industrial-financial adventures on a
global scale; retracted in the aftermath, the social plans that
condemned 50-year-old men and women to early retirement,
resulting in this astonishing statistic: even today, the average
retirement age is only 59, even though some people complain
that the legal retirement age could be "reduced" to 60.

Young people are laughing out loud at our good fortune. How
can we cope with this tsunami of pensioners? How can we keep
our social accounts in balance, especially in the midst of a crisis?
As early as 1962, the Laroque report announced the irruption of
post-war children into the social landscape. In 1989, Los Angeles
published *Age Wave,* one of the seminal books on population
ageing in industrialized countries.

In reality, our so-called gentrification (or its hypocritical
variant, "boboization") only concerns a thin social stratum.
Comfortable pensions exist, but not for everyone. Six hundred
thousand people, mostly single women, live "thanks" to the
Allocation de solidarité pour les personnes âgées (ASPA), which
amounted to 777 euros per month on April 1, 2012. The average
pension peaks at 1,200 euros. A third of women work until the
age of 65 to make up for contribution gaps due to interrupted
careers. They earn 825 euros on average. Men, 1,426 euros.
Gender inequality, even in poverty!

Our "excellent" health suffers from a few hiccups. Between
the ages of 60 and 70, we are beset by ailments that are considered benign, but very annoying. Our teeth grind and grind,
calling for heavy care, pivots or prostheses. Our eyesight
changes, forcing us to buy expensive, complex glasses, despite

the good Mr. Afflelou. Our skeleton cracks. Osteoporosis and arthrosis make us limp, rheumatism obsesses us. When we fall, we fracture. We've reached the age of physiotherapy and osteopathy appointments, spa treatments and orthopedic operations. Our tired vertebrae pinch nerves at critical, unreachable points. Sciatica, lower back pain, lumbago, cruralgia, pinched cervical vertebrae —it's time to say "ouch, ouch, ouch, Mother, what have I done to God to get here?

A study by the Institut national d'études démo graphiques (INED) sounded the alarm in 2011. It reveals "less favorable trends than in the past" in our state of health, and states that "functional and sensory limitations affect more than seven out of ten people over the age of 65, and one out of two people over the age of 50". And "cognitive limitations are not very frequent, but they are visible before the age of 60, for both men and women". Result: "These signs indicate that it will be difficult for some people to increase their overall level of activity, particularly the poorest, as social inequalities are very marked in the chances of reaching the age of 65 in good health".

My friend Mado is two years younger than me. You may not notice, but I always walk on her left.

She lacks balance. Inner ear problem. Marie-Christine has vitreous disease, a partly hereditary eye condition that sets in with age. She lives in semi-darkness, never having to look directly at the sun. Catherine was my editor-in-chief when I worked on the Ministry of Tourism newspaper. As a child and young woman, she had played the piano a lot, reaching an almost professional level. Her wish to take up music again in retirement will not be fulfilled: she has osteoarthritis in her hands. Annie would like to join the choir, but she can't hear any more. "Can't hear" is shorthand for having a whole host of parasitic sounds in the ear, some low-pitched, some high-pitched, so much so that hearing aid specialists are scrambling to find the right correction. We hear that hearing aids are advancing by leaps and bounds. This is good news, as the number of hearing aid wearers doubled between 2000 and 2011, from 250,000 to 500,000.

Arlette, "little Arlette" as we used to say at school, had breast cancer. Cured! Of course, most breast cancers are, so what's there to complain about? Wonderful reconstructive surgery even remodeled Arlette's breast, even though she's not a member of the Amazon tribe. To make this breast, muscles were pulled from her back and arm. One is shorter than the other, and all swollen. She wears tunics with wide sleeves. Arlette was delighted to learn that they no longer operate in this way.

And Bernadette, who lived for horses? She has diabetes. Falling off the nag due to hypoglycemia was out of the question. She sold her horse. She was old anyway (the mare). Positivism. Our "full fitness" is presented as self-evident, when in fact it's an arranged truth, not to say a lie.

So let's pretend, let's blush the cheeks, hide the scars, minimize. How can a woman in her sixties complain? What indecency!... This pampered generation, so well cared for, which has lacked nothing, and patati and patata.

As for our life expectancy, the spectacular figures often quoted have a major flaw, both literally and figuratively. They exclude so-called "premature" mortality. Before the age of 65, 35.9% of the population died from tumours, 15.9% from circulatory accidents. Disappearances and bereavements are knocking at our door. These are no longer exceptions or accidents, as they were when we were younger, but frequent events, all too frequent.

Let's take a step up. Dare to be sacrilegious! Let's put the infallibility of commonly accepted projections on lifespan to the test of scientific doubt. For example, let's look a little further than the tip of our nose, i.e. beyond France. In 2008, life expectancy in the United States came to a standstill for the first time since the post-war period. In addition to an inequitable healthcare system, the cause is diseases caused by obesity and smoking. Russia lost five years of life expectancy after the fall of the Berlin Wall, due to a brutal cure of liberalism. It has not recovered from this fall, despite a slight improvement.

It's not a question of playing optimism against pessimism, confidence against skepticism or vice versa, but rather of asking, with Jacques Vallin and France Meslé, in the magazine *Populations*: "Can we gain three months indefinitely?" Among the doubts they express: "Are we in the midst of a new health transition due to care for the elderly?" Gene therapy and reconstructive surgery are moving in this direction, they concede, but "will the political, economic and social changes that would enable the benefits to be distributed to all be in place?"

Alongside hard-core demography, a new generation of researchers prefers to approach aging from a biological anthropological perspective, which "relates the evolution of different body parts over time, and their pathologies, to one's professional, social and personal activities, one's physical environment, one's economic and cultural level, and social representations", as defined by Nicole Chapuis-Lucciani, Director of Research at the CNRS.

The epinal image of wealthy, fit and healthy sixty-somethings is taking a beating. An assortment of unscrupulous experts, glib journalists and other columnists pretend to believe this fable in order to impose an iron discipline on us, a mixture of hygienism and moral injunctions, the official doctrine of the Republic since the launch of the National Plan for Ageing Well (2007-2009). Initially an adverb and a verb, the expression has gradually acquired the majesty of a noun, "bienvieillir". Despite its neologism quality, which should give it momentum, the term has already congealed into a corpus of norms sillier than a gendarmerie regulation. Beware of obtuse rules. In the army, they contribute to cohesion. In our case, to keep costs down.

But I anticipate. It's only gradually that I've discovered the other side of the coin: our physical fragility denied by official doctrine, our money worries met with incredulous ears, the alternation of days when we're flattered and those when we're mortified, the mornings when we think we're 20 and those when old age already seems to be snatching us up.

Praise be to Gloria, Ovaltine, Phosphatine, the Sorbonne, May '68 and even redundancy plans and early retirement! My back is still strong enough and my mind loose enough to take it all in stride. The columnists will get their money's worth. Well, almost. I sometimes fall into their trap, because I'm still a bit naive (I didn't experience the rigors of war, so please go back to the beginning).

Here, then, is the true story of my adventures and those of many of my companions in the land of Sexagenia, and of the surprising discoveries we made there.

Chapter II
Retirement at 60

Yesterday, on the transatlantic liners, a shower of fireworks illuminated the passage of the Line. Champagne was flowing. The orchestra played the foxtrot and the mambo. Today, the traveler follows the miniature silhouette of a plane on the flight map with a jaded eye. Without warning, it lands like a fly on the line separating the two hemispheres. No one notices, unless a slightly poetic captain coughs into his microphone to announce, in his reassuring bass voice, that "our aircraft has just crossed the Equator".

And so it is with the famous 60-year old retirement age, from which we would be the beneficiaries. This "line" has been in a state of flux since the 2003 reform, which extended the legal contribution period for salaried workers, and therefore for certain sexas, by one quarter a year. What's more —but this is not part of the myth— retirement was already staggered, since the "regimes" for shopkeepers, craftsmen, farmers, self-employed workers and a few other professions provide for retirement at 65 or even 67. A pretext for the latter to fulminate against the "privileges" of salaried workers. Except that early retirements due to the numerous redundancy plans devised since the first oil crisis have added to the confusion, if not outright redundancies of people in their fifties who can't find new jobs.

It's hardly surprising, then, that leaving the company is no longer done, as it used to be (or as, perhaps, it is in the collective imagination), with drums and trumpets.

When I liquidated my pension, nothing happened. I had found an alternative, the status of micro-entrepreneur, compatible with an activity below a certain sales ceiling, and with no "discount" to boot. This choice enabled me to reduce my activity smoothly while still drawing my pension. A very favorable situation, I must admit! This combination is a sweet treat that the law grants to those who are willing to work beyond the legal retirement age.

Curious language, isn't it? These words *pension, liquidate, rating, discount, full rate, accumulation.* Pure notary's or insurer's grimoire. You'll need to immerse yourself in this vocabulary when preparing for your retirement, if you haven't already done so. It's an old-fashioned dictionary where *toucher* doesn't mean "to touch money", but "to receive a bank transfer", where *régime* designates the contribution and departure terms for a professional category, where *cote* and *décote* mean a percentage more or less than the basic scheme and where *cumuler* has nothing infamous about it. An astonishing world that, for me, has a taste of Vichy pastille (because of the regime). When I read "pension", "for retirement", I think of some low-cost spa treatment. Maybe because of the Vichy water. Or boarding houses.

But let's not get carried away with the sweets and frills. It's true that a lot of employees my age have retired (what greed in the verb, suddenly!) at 60 on the dot. One such lucky man, who young people talk about with lust, will have organized a farewell party in meeting room C 38, listened —moved like a kid at the prize-giving— to the laudatory speech of his boss/supervisor/ boss/manager/boss, to which he will have replied with a kind word, albeit peppered with well-measured jabs. His colleagues will have chipped in to buy him a present. A tennis racket or a set of golf clubs for a man, jewelry, a scarf, a book (*La Retraite heureuse*) or a gardening kit for a woman.

The next day, he or she will have opened their eyes in astonishment (didn't the alarm go off?), and thought they were on vacation. A feeling of unparalleled euphoria will have overtaken him or her when they realize that never again, until... well, for a very long time.

Eager to make the most of it, our man —yesterday in a suit and tie, today in Bermuda polo shorts— sets off on a cruise to Coconut *Island*. Informed of his birthday, the captain invites him to his table. For dessert, the waiters bring a cake with sixty lit candles. He blows them out as the captain toasts, "To your new youth, Monsieur Benoît!" Transpose to the feminine for a lady, replacing the suit with a suit, the Bermuda shorts with Bermuda shorts.

"New youth." It's not just a table talk. Go to any bookshop and you'll see books with unequivocal titles: *La vie commence à la retraite, La Retraite, un nouveau départ, Enfin la vraie vie!* Wouldn't it be more accurate to speak of a new stage in the continuity of life? Sociologist Bernard Arcand remarks: "Old age is a section of life that only has meaning in relation to what precedes it. The third age will take on its meaning in relation to the other ages of life, and the treatment reserved for old age must be coherent with what society defines as childhood and adulthood". This man talks gold, but is hardly listened to...

But let's not spoil the fun for our pensioner on his way to the islands...

After sailing the turquoise seas, our friend returns home one day (unless he's one of the few who set down their trunks elsewhere). He then experiences a kind of depression, similar to the baby-blues of young mothers. So he says to himself: *what if I drop in to see my colleagues?* He walks through the door, all happy, with his travel photos. Gudule is in a meeting. The boss gives her a hurried wave: "Come back on Tuesday, it's quieter. Yes, at the cafet." Annie... "Where's Annie?" "She's having a makeover," murmurs Sonia. Annie, back from the bathroom, has pink lips. "Oh, Julien, how nice of you to come and see us! I'm just giving you a little kiss because I've got an appointment with a customer..."

Julien leaves, disappointed. Do you get a lot of retired people coming into your company to say hello? Yes, they come by. Once, twice, at most. In any case, with the *turnover...* They don't know anyone anymore.

Back to the pot. The farewell drink. I notice that it's a rarity. Marine, my cousin, is a nurse. She has spent her entire career in the same hospital. When she tells me she's leaving, I exclaim:

- You're going to make one hell of a pot, I suppose!

- No pot.

I must be deaf.

- How do you say, no pot?

- No luck. Nada, niet.

- Huh?

- No, I don't want any pot. The good times are over. No more staff friendship. Every man for himself. I'm inviting a few good friends to dinner. And two nice doctors.

Nadine, hairdresser. "You don't even think about it! I've already had a hard enough time keeping up, with all those young girls pushing you out the door..." Agnès, editorial secretary. "I was lucky enough not to be laid off. There's no more SR. Journalists have become versatile, multimedia! My editor-in-chief looks at me like I've got nothing to do. The worst thing is that it's becoming true! So I'm leaving. I've negotiated a severance package. I'm going to evaporate quietly..."

In their book, *Les Baby-boomers: une génération mobile*, Catherine Bonvalet and Jeffrey Sachs identify this fragmentation of departures, which they group into four groups: those who enjoyed a stable working life right up to the end, those whose rectilinear careers came to a screeching halt due to early retirement, those who suffered career gaps due to either prolonged unemployment or long-term illness, and the fourth group who alternated phases of salaried work, unemployment, intermittent work, vacations, self-employment or semi-independence. Just like me. Or like Andrée, who became a single mother of a disabled child at the age of 23. Her career? Temporary work, more temporary work, and a few fixed-term contracts. Andrée has seen a lot of the country! She's worked at TF1, in banking, fashion and agriculture. She knows women who have worked like her, getting by as best they can. One friend, a hairdresser at Alexandre's who brushed the stars, fell on hard times. Another, a dancer at Crazy Horse. At 65, she lives on the minimum old-age pension.

After all, you may say, stopping work is just a social marker, and it's not unpleasant to cross the threshold gently. However, there's something unsettling about the absence of boundaries, especially when the increasingly stealthy departure is preceded (or followed) by a very discreet sixtieth birthday. Many of my friends consider it tactless to wish a loved one a happy 60th. Worse still! Some of my friends, intoxicated by the prevailing youthism, demand that this unfortunate day be made a thing of the past.

Don't talk about it, no one will see it? Naive superstition! The 60-something, retired or about to be, looks at himself in the mirror: "Mirror, my beautiful mirror, am I still young?" He's perplexed. A trivial event makes him realize the tipping point.

This is what happened to me when I inadvertently introduced myself as "retired" to a group of young journalists to whom I was teaching the basics of the profession. The reaction could be read in the sulky expressions on their faces: oh dear, a disconnected old fart, what is she going to teach us... the conjugation of the past perfect subjunctive? I quickly caught up with the situation, specifying "retired for the sake of it, because I'm a micro-entrepreneur" (Phew!) Entrepreneur, even a micro-entrepreneur, is quite something.

You love your job and want to organize a farewell party, even though you've been made redundant? Plan it! You're leaving in the right way, at the right age, but you don't want to listen to the hypocritical speech of a superior who's delighted to get rid of you? Organize it outside the walls, like my cousin. The atmosphere at work has deteriorated, solidarity is on the wane, and a new generation has no chemistry with you? Be content with a courteous e-mail, if you think that'll bring things full circle. In short, act according to your whim, your heart, your free will!

However, in the name of realism, which you may consider to be self-indulgent, I would advise against leaving your bag unpacked, except in extreme cases, because these days you never know what might happen.

Maybe tomorrow, your employer will ask you to come back for a fixed-term contract tutoring action.

Chapter III
Our Properties

I collapse on a hammock, hastily hung. Eight hours of driving behind me. Unloading luggage, opening doors and shutters, plugging in the fridge, turning on the water supply, a trip to the supermarket, unpacking groceries, climbing the stepladder to get sheets out of the big wardrobe, bed made. Phew!

I smoke, I rest. As I have every year since I split my time between Paris and the Drôme, opening the country house wears me out. "Double residency is all the rage", says a recent issue of *Notre Temps*. Above all, it's exhausting.

A mosquito attacks me, then two, then three. I forgot to buy tortillas. It's chilly in the house. I'll have to add another blanket.

Last year, I prepared a feast of regional specialties. Tonight, chicken wings from the supermarket will do the trick. Last year, I listened to my favorite CD. This year, my ears are too tired to appreciate the music. Last year, I sorted the damp mail. This year, I'm brushing it off with a wave of my hand. There's nothing in that pile of envelopes that can't wait.

I take a drag on my cigarette, inert and with my eyes closed.

Zen attitude? Not at all! I'm trapped in a web of anguish.

How could I have asked my parents to give me this large building? By what aberration have I allowed myself to be taken in by the galimatias of notaries on "optimizing inheritance tax"? To be an owner, that I am. With all the consequences for my bank account. I'll never get out of it. Where am I going to get the money? A second home is expensive. What madness! What about the pool? The pool is 30 years old. It doesn't filter well, the paint is peeling, the coping is loosening. And the well pump, so fragile? Has the pump given up the ghost?

The mention of the broken-down pump pulls me out of the hammock. I head for the cellar. I plug in the plug above which is written "pump". Suspense: it sputters. And off it goes. Phew!

Once upstairs, I take a tour of the garden. The irises are exploding, the peonies are opening, the rosebuds are about to bloom, a forest of daffodils is colonizing the banks of the stream, and the meadow is dotted with daisies. It's so beautiful here, and smells so good! Refreshed, I decide to build a fire in the fireplace. Back to the cellar for a few logs. I choose five large ones and three medium ones. Heavy stuff. In the middle of the staircase, I lose my balance. Badaboum! My load collapses. My back is killing me. I stretch before picking up the scattered wood, scramble back upstairs and finally light a nice fire.

Let's not complain! I'm part of the tiny minority who can, as people say, "afford" a double residence. At a time when young adults are forced to move back in with their parents because they can't afford the rent, it's a luxury. I'm free to sell this country house, after all. Oh, not very expensively, because I'd have to redo the electrical panel, insulate the roof, put in double windows, change the boiler, asphalt the access road full of holes —in other words, "work to be planned", as the estate agent will write. My children would be very sad, because this is a refuge, a place of memories.

But I said I wouldn't complain, since I own two residences, which puts me among the "privileged". You should know that 74% of senior citizens own their own homes. We told you they were rich... Well, for Andrée, it's the end of the statistics. At 65, she sold her apartment. She could no longer afford the utilities. She found a shared apartment for old people in Pantin, on the other side of the Paris ring road. This type of collective housing for retired people is "emerging", I read on the Agevillage website, one of the leading sites on our age (which I'll talk about later).

Marine, my nurse cousin, the one who didn't want to have a farewell party at her company, has plans: she'd like to sell her apartment in the Lyon suburbs because it's home to noisy, violent and dangerous gangsters. Estimated value: 110,000 euros. With this sum, where to buy, and what? The city center is out of reach, as are the green hills of the Monts du Lyonnais. Prospecting in Valence, to be seen...

Ah, we're making real estate projects! Castles, bastides, ruins languishing in ivy and restored at great expense, waterfront villas, private beachfronts, we tell you, we're varnished. Some of us. For the others, the little two-roomed flat, the three-roomed flat that smells of decay. It's better, we say. My kind of women who think they can keep a big house in the country, they're cicadas, they're short-sighted, especially if they don't have a husband (no husband means only one pension). Wise women and their partners make strategic withdrawals in due course, carefully thought out with the architect and gerontologist. If their house is big, they sell it for a smaller one. It's sad, but it has to be, as Gertrude writes (with tears in her eyes) on Aménagement-construction.com:

"We're building a single-storey house on land we own, but it's heartbreaking to have to sell the one the children grew up in! Gertrude can console herself. The new house will have inclined surfaces to slide the wheelchair into, a kitchen calibrated to allow it to turn, an opening bathtub, a Stannah stairlift, Everstyl armchairs and weights under the carpets. A real hospital, but cosy. With favorite paintings and family photos. Because, you see, autonomy in housing, as elsewhere, is not in the mind. Of course not! It's a question of equipment, of robotics in a way. For machine-men.

The "concept" of a home for senior citizens is reassuring in its enormity. It seems that "serviced residences" in the Hespérides or Senioriales style are not very popular with the 55-69 age bracket, except for a few sites near the Côte d'Azur. Builders are therefore falling back on the single-family home and home equipment market. Proof that we're not in it for the long haul, or that we're not as rich as the *senior marketing* pundits had hoped.

Chapter IV
Their Big Bucks

Puberty is a time of many "firsts" for a young girl: first period, first nightclubbing, first joint, first embrace, who knows? Less well known are the "first times" of a woman celebrating her 60th birthday.

Here's a cruel one. Imagine your local convenience store. Around 7 p.m., the store is packed. Customers are anxious to get home, catch their commuter train, rest their feet or just relax. Exasperation builds to the point of riot.

What does this have to do with old age? Be patient!

I avoid shopping at this infernal hour. However, one Thursday, after going to the cinema in the morning, I go to the mini-market.

Clack! The trap is closing. I walk for twenty minutes before I reach the checkout.

The employee asks me for 7.35 euros. I'm about to hand her a 10-euro bill, when I realize I might have the extra. I put my wallet back in my bag and take out my purse. This permutation, five seconds at most, provokes a nervous spasm that runs the length of the tail's spine.

Under the benevolent gaze of the "cashier", always short of yellow coins, I explore my reticule. I find not 7.35 euros, but

8.40 euros. Patricia (says her name tag) shudders. The subtraction frightens her, despite the machine.

A concert of onomatopoeia explodes: grrrr, pssssss, ibcile, viokk, jpaksaafair... Panicked, the girl grabs my wallet, pours out the contents, takes four 2 euro coins that make 8, plus two 20 centime coins that make 40 and gives me back 1 euro and 5 centimes.

I humbly put my change away. Wrathful brow furrows. "Another old woman who can't count. - Her eyesight is so poor she can't make out the yellow coins. - I bet she confuses euros with francs, and even old francs, if that's possible." For a first time, that's one!

Moral: never let a cashier rummage through your wallet. Hold it firmly at arm's length. Present a bill for an amount exceeding the amount due with a straight face.

The recipe is not infallible. Some people use it as an excuse to grumble: "What selfish old hides! Do you think they'd bother to top up? You should see them take out their 50s. With their fat pensions, they don't give a damn about the cost of living! In this country, there's only enough for the old!"

Chapter V
They Think They Can Do Anything

The butcher is between two wines. Whether by deliberate choice or as a result of his alcoholic impregnation, he has adopted the populo style.

I order three osso buco and a marrow bone.

Butcher (*jovial*):

- So you're going to make a veal stock?

- I'd like a marrow bone, please.

Butcher (*staggering*):

- Yes, but are you going to make a veal stock for your osso?

- Monsieur, it's been three generations since women cooked gravy. Neither do restaurateurs, for that matter. Marrow is for spreading on croutons, if you must know.

Butcher (*not listening*):

- It's not difficult, little lady. For a veal stock, you boil the bones with a small onion, some thyme, two cloves, skim and reduce.

Me (*annoyed*):

- You can't teach me how to make veal stock! That's not the point. You don't need veal stock for an osso buco.

Butcher (*hug*):

- In that case, I'd love to be in your kitchen to see how you cook... Would you ever invite me?

Me (*exasperated*):

- Look, I just want a bone marrow.

Him (*sharp*):

- Well, I don't have any! Besides, you old-timers have your recipes, but they've fallen by the wayside.

Me (*resigned*):

- Then give me three slices of ribeye.

Him (*smiling*):

- There you go! We're getting reasonable. So, the rib-eye, just pan-fried, top and bottom, a touch of fresh butter and parsley. I say, 620 grams, 39.60 euros.

Overpriced! I leave, furious. He hails me.

- Hey, lady, you forgot your merchandise!

I go home and bury the package in my cart.

Butcher (*between his teeth*):

- These old spinning tops, they forget everything. And they yell at you, too. They think they can do anything."

It's just that, after 60, people don't like us to "know how" to cook, love, raise children, insulate the house, read an estimate...

We're suddenly presumed impotent and ignorant, and therefore pretentious, when we share our experience. At best, we're listened to gently. "He (she) knows nothing. He (she) has old methods, old techniques, obsolete know-how." Add to this an awkward house, with no double windows or aluminum shutters, cluttered with old furniture and tired armchairs.

And yet, we think we're the masters of the world, with our advice, our condescension, even our arrogance. When it comes to driving, "old" people our age think they can do anything. The “old” ones are the real deal! You can spot them at a glance, with their seats against the steering wheel, their tense arms, their glasses, their squeaky gears, their handbrake on at the drop of a hat, their notorious incompetence at traffic circles. Well, they're happy to grumble when you honk at them behind their backs because they don't start fast enough at a green light.

Chapter VI
They Know Nothing About Computers

At the *L'Automne heureuse* computer club, the bickering goes on and on, like fowl fighting in a henhouse.

The geological stratification between eras of our initiations is a hellish cause of spats. MS-DOS is at loggerheads with the antediluvian followers of an even more cabalistic language: Fortran. Fans of the late Atari insist that nothing has ever matched the musical performance of this brand; the duel between PC and Mac rages on; among grandparents, jet lag imposes its rhythm. Mémé is frantic not to miss the opportunity to laugh with Gaëlle (three months old) in her nursery in Nouméa. Monsieur Gastinois, a distinguished professor of geography, has a workstation to himself all evening. Thanks to Google Earth, he is trying to unravel the mystery of the sources of the Orinoco. He forbids anyone to occupy his seat for even half an hour. Science first!

"Rude! Selfish! Enquiquineur! Unlearned!" shouted the grandmothers. Henri Gastinois, a grandfather, retorted: "Silence, you ignorant old spinning tops. To your knitting!" One day, when Hélène Bridou insisted on taking his place, he slapped her across the face. The police came very close.

In this witch's cauldron, a few 60-somethings are content to master the basics. Alas, even these modest applicants have to contend with chattemite. The ex-stenodactylos laugh under their breath at the distressing spectacle of the two-fingered men. They remind them all too much of their former bosses! The Pivot dictation enthusiasts take offence at those who get lost in the maze of pronominal verbs, and scornfully send them back to their Bescherelle. Keeping a cool head in these conditions is a real feat. I deserted after five sessions.

"We don't see you at the club anymore," says a surprised Hélène Bridou, whom I meet at the post office.

I'm reluctant to admit to him that I'm now taking private lessons to fill the gaps left by my work as a journalist, because I've used my computer like a typewriter keyboard and am only comfortable in Word.

"I've given up. I'm too old. All these clicks are real mouse traps."

To think that these gray-haired kids deplore the fact that our schoolchildren are impossible to keep up with. "We've got to keep them in line!" They'd be well advised to take the lesson to heart. What this club needs is a well-informed teacher, coupled with a dragon capable of imposing iron discipline on these unrepentant brawlers.

The truth is, as I later realized, that this club is only for the truly ignorant 60-somethings. Most are tech-savvy and well-equipped. In 2000, there were over a million Internet users between the ages of 50 and 64, and only 147,000 over 65. Today, 60-69 year-olds are equipped and connected like the average population. Sales of simplified computers, such as Ordissimo, are marking time. In fact, we're virtuosos, papys-surfers. At least for those who have had a taste of computers at work. There are even ordimaniacs and iPad wizards among us. But that doesn't mean there aren't arguments about the screen. With family and friends, the insults fly. We're incorrigible.

CHAPTER VII
CAN BABY PET THE DOG?

On Sunday afternoons in my chic neighborhood, young adults in designer sportswear stroll down Avenue du Château with their families. I walk my dog Rac in jeans and a big, comfortable sweater.

As I pass the adorable faces of children and plump newborns, I melt with tenderness. I want to caress the round cheek of the baby, pick up the comforter that's fallen on the floor, send back the stray ball.

Beware of following these innocent (im)impulses! You'll be stunned in the moment by chilling stares.

I pick up a teddy bear in disarray in the alley and hand it to its owner in a stroller. This gesture is vigorously intercepted. Mom and Dad are thinking about germs, bacteria and allergies. They dust the teddy carefully before handing it back to their little Lucas.

What's this stranger got to do with anything? These grannies, what do they know about children, eh? Do they? Big deal. Kids raised in communities in the Ardèche, surrounded by cigarette smoke and pot... Suddenly, the mother realizes that I'm not the post-68 type. That's obvious, because I don't wear purple sarouels. So I'm one of those old ladies who gives out sweets packed with calories and additives, who goes "guili, guili", and sings *Ma dent, ma petite dent* by Henri Dès. A corny category, but less dangerous than the first.

She's at that point in her deductions, when Lucas asks, "Can I pet the little dog?" The kid insists, bordering on the whimsical. Tempest under the parents' skulls. The husband calls up memories of his personal development course, "Be responsive in all circumstances". He mentally makes two columns, the "pros" and the "cons".

For:

- It's not a hound.

- It is kept on a leash.

- Contact with animals fosters children's psycho-affective development.

Against:

- Isn't it permissive to give in to Lucas?

- I cannot be certain that the vaccinations are up to date.

- Lucas's arm gesture may scare the dog into biting to defend itself.

Three against three. A draw. Distraught, the father consults the mother. I can tell from her attitude that Mum is arguing "for". What I don't know is that she secretly wants to own a Yorkie.

Dad cuts the Gordian knot. "Lucas, you just pet the dog a little bit on the top of the head." Green light. I take three steps forward. Lucas advances his handcuff towards the hairball: "Easy, Lucas, easy! He might bite you." Mom gave in to emotion. Lucas, frightened, bursts into tears.

I move on. Ten meters further on, I come across a baby who is laughing and laughing and bubbling and bubbling at his doting mother. I lean over to the little wonder. The mother speeds up in panic. Could she have mistaken me for a child stealer?

I slow down, confused. Introspection. Am I becoming paranoid? I'm not so sure. Seeing me gazing greedily at their little ones, the parents might guess that I'm a lady in need of grandchildren.

Chapter VIII
They Forgot Everything

"How thoughtless!" I take a bounty tone, as if I'd forgotten a detail, even though I've made a big blunder.

Imagine the scene: I got up at 5 a.m. in the country, got ready in fifteen minutes, jumped into my Twingo, then onto the TGV, caught the metro, to find myself at precisely 8.45 a.m. at the foot of the training center where I teach in Paris, thanks to my retired self-employed status. On the menu: a two-day course on professional writing. I greet Patricia, the receptionist.

- Hi, Pat. What room am I in?

She consults her schedule and raises an eyebrow:

- I can't see you.

I'm standing in front of her, aren't I? I suggest she check. After a brief check, she murmurs:

- Those are the dates, but next month.

I take the uppercut. I got a month wrong. The hostess is sorry.

- Rest a while. Would you like some coffee or orange juice?

- No, thanks, I've just had breakfast. So, until next time, the good one!

With that, I burst out laughing and set off.

She certainly felt sorry for herself. You should never inspire pity when you get old. Damn, damn and damn! I collapse on the terrace of a café, order a double express, devastated. I haven't even saved face. Yet it's easy to suggest that, between the invitation e-mail and the usual confirmations, a "quality incident" may have infiltrated the computer chain.

I brood over my disappointment. The coffee tastes like defeat. The street is sinister. Not a cat to be seen, except some bloated night owls on their way home. Will I leave Paris defeated, humiliated?

Minutes pass. The sun comes out. It's a pleasant terrace. I order a croissant. What if I went to the cinema? A newsagent pulls up his gate. On *Pariscope*, I choose *Gran Torino*, 11 a.m. showing. The show puts me in a good mood. As a retired boxer, Clint Eastwood is more seductive than ever.

At the exit, summer heat. Tourists walk in tight rows, Parisians work languidly. The tar melts, the sky is flag-blue. I go to a restaurant, then visit an exhibition on the travel diaries of writers and painters. Sketches, drawings, quotations, watercolors, poems...

On the way out, my misadventure seems a long way off. After all, no one was harmed except me. No trainee has been deprived of an internship. The company's top executives are in the Luberon. I didn't put a dent in sales.

This non-existent internship is really "zero defects". I'm thrilled to have found this joke. What to do after the exhibition? I visit one of my sons. I spend some time chatting in his garden. The last TGV has left. I return to my winter home to spend the night. I think it looks nice in summer clothes. I stay one more day, playing the provincial girl on vacation in Paris.

On the return journey, as the train speeds through the Mâcon-Loché area, I replay the events of the day. It's true, I make more mistakes in my various appointments than I used to. I also forget. The horrifying sword of Damocles that is Alzheimer's hangs over me. My friends and I often talk about it, and play a game of ooh, ooh, scare me: "I've got my keys, I've got my shrink's appointment, I've got my wallet, I've got my bread at the baker's, I've got Post-it notes everywhere…".

Memory lapses? Yes. But that doesn't mean you have to rush off to do crosswords and sudoku puzzles, sign up for bridge or recite poetry. The new disease of the century (along with cancer, stroke and a few others) has a very nice ring to it. It refers to so many different lesions, visible or not on an MRI scan, and presents so many variations, that I've come to think of it as nothing more than the inevitable cerebral aging that affects us all to a greater or lesser extent. We feed our fear with the sight of our parents, when they are still alive.

"My mother has Alzheimer's." It's the absolute horror, the supreme degradation, the decline, almost a disgrace. Well, at the nursing home where I visit her, I find that my mother has happy Alzheimer's. She only remembers what suits her. She only remembers what suits her.

Chapter IX
"Their" Andropause

- Mine is unbearable.

- Mine too. He doesn't want to go out anymore. Stays in his chair for hours.

What's wrong with their dogs, I wonder, listening to Christine and Marie-Claire.

- Are your doggies tired?

(*Laughter in chorus*).

- It's not our dogs we're talking about, it's our husbands. It's because of their andropause.

I'm stunned. I live alone, which perhaps explains my reaction. I certainly thought that, when we reached a certain age, our husbands and partners had what we call "breakdowns" more often than in the past. And I naively imagined that, thanks to Viagra®, everything was back to normal.

No, no, no, my friends explained. Viagra® isn't that simple. You have to seize the moment, between the ingestion of the pill and the moment of its effect, for the prelude. It's quite an art, they explained.

The blue pill isn't as miraculous as I thought. Sometimes its active molecule, sildenafil citrate, doesn't do the trick. Transdermal patches must then be applied to the trunk, stomach and thighs. Worse still, the Muse. This micro-pellet to be inserted into the urethra provides inspiration. The medical panoply also includes venous slowing devices, surgical implants and penile injections, all of which are painful and humiliating treatments. The more lenient Androgel® 2% concentrate and Testim® 1% concentrate should only be prescribed in the event of a proven drop in testosterone levels.

It has long been thought that this hormone decreases in our companions in very small steps, based on the observation that very old men can be fathers. An American study, the *European male aging study*, published in 2010, claims that testosterone decline affects only 2% of men between the ages of 40 and 80, and 3% between the ages of 60 and 69. These figures are highly contested. The monthly magazine *Notre temps* claims that 25% of men experience a sex hormone deficiency after the age of 50, a figure echoed by Dr. Mimoun, a friendly sexologist who reports on France 5. In the United States, a wind of panic is blowing. Testosterone intake by these gentlemen has increased twenty-fold in twenty years.

Whatever the precise rate of evolution of the male hormone, women have a crucial role to play when it comes to taps. The Doctissimo website puts it poetically: "Ladies, help them get back on track!" And it adds that "women too often have a castrating attitude", whereas they need to "find the right words", because "this problem must be shared within the couple".

Well, it had better be. Otherwise, beware! Dr. Ian Banks warns: "Some disorders stem from the onset of menopause in the partner, upsetting the couple's bearings."

So we shouldn't be surprised if, as the superlative doctor states, "13% of men have tried to reassure themselves by entering into a relationship with another partner".

Christine is one of them. Her husband has repeatedly reassured himself. At 74, the old lion has admitted defeat. So he returned home, where my Penelope of Christine used to be. Marie-Dominique had no such patience. She filed for divorce, much to the incomprehension of her children.

Because andropause is not just a sexual disorder. It affects mood. That's what Christine and Marie-Claire were talking about. In addition to reduced libido, other symptoms affect older males. Hot flushes, night sweats, fatigue, vague depression, slight memory and concentration problems, I read on PasseportSanté.net.

Diabetics argue about whether these inconveniences are a consequence of reduced sexual appetite or an intrinsic manifestation. It's the 21st-century lung controversy. They suggest that cigarettes, alcohol, marijuana, cholesterol and excess weight don't help. They are unlikely to be contradicted. Sitting can, they warn, "reduce vascularization". A finding that fits in perfectly with the advice, repeatedly given to sexas, to walk for at least an hour a day. More surprisingly, cycling is said to have a negative impact on erectile capacity "beyond three hours a week". Men will therefore prefer jogging or swimming. When it comes to virility, the best is sometimes the enemy of the good. Propecia®, prescribed for baldness, is said to promote erectile difficulties.

Note that many of the disorders described by PasseportSanté are "mild" or "vague". Admire the understatement. It's intended to distinguish andropause from menopause. An abyss, indeed, a gulf, separates them!

"Unlike women, men don't have a clear-cut milestone such as the cessation of menstruation" pouts Wikipedia (net, you bet...), followed by the incorrigible Doctissimo: "The reality of the menopause is indisputable. On the other hand, many specialists doubt that men experience an equivalent phenomenon, since androgen secretion never really stops." PasseportSanté.net concludes: "There are no symptoms other than those associated with aging, obesity or other health problems."

As a result, the relevance of the term *andropause* is "questioned". Some prefer the term *climatère masculin*, to suggest a gentle slope. We also say *androclise*. More scientifically, *hypoglandism*. Martial acronyms such as DAP (partial androgen deficiency) and DALA (age-related androgen deficiency) are in vogue. *DALA* sounds good, and is less ugly than *menopause*.

DO THIS, DON'T DO THAT

Chapter X
Our Coaches

To help us stay in shape, we employ coaches. Our good retreats allow us this luxury. Under the term *"coach,"* I include once and for all, so as not to repeat myself, sexagenics experts of all calibers, physiotherapists, osteopaths, rheumatologists, gastroenterologists, proctologists, dentists, odontologists, opticians and audioprosthetists, psychologists and psychotherapists of all persuasions, gerontologists, yoga, calisthenics, Pilates, kung fu and shiatsu teachers, dieticians, pastors, monks and priests, as well as those who serve as their mouthpieces in magazines, radio and TV programs, on the Web and in printed books, plus all those I'm forgetting.

At our age, employing a personal trainer is really a luxury. All you need to do is subscribe to *Pleine vie*, watch the *ad hoc* column on France 5's *Magazine de la Santé* (conveniently right after the 1 p.m. news) or browse through a bookshop.

I've made some astonishing discoveries: these great pedagogues usually group their advice into three, five, seven or ten precepts, a mnemonic architecture of numbers that may even be biblical, cabalistic or apocalyptic in inspiration, with a dash of behaviorism, a science inclined to distinguish a precise number of stages in "self-fulfillment" (which I call "mental training").

Pierre Vinot, author of *Petit traité pour réussir sa retraite* (*A treatise on successful retirement*), sums up his comments around seven guidelines. I can't resist the pleasure of quoting the first three.

1 - Look after our appearance. Let's look younger, with our hair, clothes and glasses.

2 - Let's beware of long, frustrating gaps (according to the author, "non-activity generates non-time").

3 - We're going to have health problems. We must never talk about it, not even to our nearest and dearest.

How about that! Mr. doesn't talk to anyone about his prostate, and suffers in the toilet, while Mrs. stands stiff as a board when urine leakage is imminent and her only recourse is to wet her underpants through the Téna protection, of which all models, even the most resistant, even those with side ties, are porous...

Aimable Vinot takes us back to the heyday of Puritanism! Lessons in deportment, facade impassivity, is this the modernity of aging well? Not a word, not a complaint. What a brave old lady, what a dignified old gentleman! You know, those people who, not so long ago, humiliated their servants, fucked the maids, beat the dog and swatted the children...

There's something less crass, if I may say so. Sophie Muffang in a book with a promising title: *La retraite? Pas si simple! Comment passer le cap* (*Retirement? Not so easy! How to get through it*), invites us to calculate our stress level for the year using the Holmes-Rahe scale, based on the number of upsets we've experienced (I was too lazy, I confess, to climb the scale): we'll then know how likely we are, over the next two years, to fall ill. Forty-three life events were described by five thousand patients in 1967 as stress factors. Psychiatrists Holmes and Rahe assigned them a coefficient. For example, pregnancy is 40, the death of a spouse is 100. Write down your own, multiply by the number of times, add up. Verdict: above 300, you have a very high risk of illness, below 150, a very low one. Ah, the delights of scoring in the evening! Adapted to a PlayStation, this could be a great idea for a Christmas present, don't you think?

Another game is the two-column game. Very popular for making decisions (as used by this young father when deciding whether or not to allow his child to pet my dog), this game is suitable for a thousand situations: cases of conscience, self or other evaluations, torments of the heart... Thanks to its simplicity, which surpasses that of Sudoku, it is ideal for the elderly. In one column, you put your handicaps, in the other your assets. For example, on the left: I'm shy; on the right: I'm perseverant. Add them up.

If you have more strengths than weaknesses, congratulations! All you have to do is turn your weaknesses into strengths. In this way, the shy person will be a serious and precise interlocutor, unlike the conceited person who runs the risk of being over-confident.

If your weaknesses exceed your strengths, congratulations all the same! (Our mentors practice positive reinforcement, i.e. they always praise us, just as we should encourage our dog when he brings the ball back). You'll "just" have to cultivate your strengths and work around your weaknesses. For a sixty-something, this might mean, for example: strong point, I'm still attractive; weak point, I have erectile dysfunction. Solution: take Viagra, congratulations!

This method is used quite officially to assess the degree of autonomy of the oldest-old. The Aggir grid, a set of questions put to the supposedly spoiled, is supplemented by an interview with the neuropsychiatrist and psychomotor tests, resulting in a score on a scale of 1 to 7. I witnessed my mother's "girage". Well, the first part, because I was asked to leave afterwards. The coordinating doctor rightly whispered to me that my presence might jeopardize the scientific neutrality of the verdict. My mother was "girée" 3. As a result, her dependency benefit is very low. This financial aid for home hospitalization or nursing home rent is indexed to the Aggir grid. Mum would have had to add to her mental debility or uncontrolled hand movements.

Counting and calibration of all kinds are recommended today. Precise measuring tools are a must. Tensiometers, heart rate monitors and, above all, body mass index (BMI) scales. You see, it's absolutely essential to calculate BMI, because old-fashioned "gross" weight (in kilograms) is not enough for a "fine-tuned" approach. No fat, no fat, because lean is life! A small deviation can compromise our fitness and health.

When our coaches sign books, on the back cover, where a short biography of the author is sketched out, I often read: "lecturer in management at...", "former HRD of...", "published numerous works on team leadership and human relations..." Because our consultants, too, are retiring. Like us, they're looking for ways to make ends meet. Retraining to manage older people is an advantageous idea in every sense of the word.

Real or virtual, it works. Among the Internet addresses dedicated to my sexas friends is Agevillage, launched in 2000 by Anne de Vivie, CEO of Eternis, the company that publishes the site. It's teeming with ideas, tips and even in-depth articles. Eternis runs the Gineste Marescotti institutes, named after the "inventor" of a concept known as "humanitude". Basically, *care* refers to charity in action, and humanitude to the virtue of charity. Both terms became popular after the discovery of sad cases of mistreatment in retirement homes. Modern" thinkers are reluctant to use the secular word "*charity*" to designate palliatives to the perverse consequences of our globalized world.

What's my point? Ah, yes! Agevillage. Among the backers of this site are my colleague Yves Mamou, director of Eternis, and Jean-Louis Rochard, managing director of Praesta France, a company specializing in executive coaching. No scoop, no conflict of interest as far as I can see (I haven't investigated). This example "just" shows how corporate management methods, which we thought we'd escaped when we retired, are coming back with a vengeance to govern the time we have left in our lives. Fittingly, the site in question sums up its editorial line in the form of the "five pillars of ageing well". These people are incorrigible...

If I haven't discouraged you from taking on a coach, do something big: sign up for a course on aging well. Almost twenty years ago, I witnessed an event that I pride myself on having sniffed out as a harbinger (I'm a journalist, so I have to have flair). At the time, I was training staff for France Télécom's in-house newsletters. These monthly bulletins were called *Fréquences*. There was one for each department. When the company's capital was opened up (the privatization that didn't have a name), management encouraged agents to take "spontaneous" early retirement. Applicants were invited to participate "on a voluntary basis" in "retirement preparation courses". How humane of the company to provide future ex-employees with a viaticum to help them on their journey to non-employment!

Courses of this kind are trying to break into the training market. My pension fund offers such courses, as described in the "Revival" chapter. Apparently, they are not very successful. Good news at last! Too bad for the nice organizers... It's a case of who's got what, but that's what happens sometimes.

Chapter XI
The Benefits of Sport

A friend from work suggests I accompany her to water aerobics. At 32, she's severely overweight.

His proposal catches me off guard. Usually, at the pool, I walk haughtily past where the grannies are shaking their withered limbs to a disco tune. Little wrinkled heads under bathing caps, they try to follow the orders of a lifeguard who barks more than he speaks, coming and going over the edge like a wild animal in rut. Satisfied with my thirty "all-swimming" lengths and twenty "finning" lengths, I step lightly into the VIP area to sweat in the sauna and splash around in the Jacuzzi.

But I'm touched by my friend's request. Why not, if it will help this little girl lose weight? I agree.

Astonishment! In the very first class, I have to stop, panting, at number 16, the series entitled: "And to finish, thirty lifts on the arms at the edge of the pool, and thirty and twenty-nine and twenty-eight, come on, let's pull ourselves up high, I want to see your breasts, ladies, push harder on the forearms, you'll sleep well tonight."

French fries can play tricks on me, because underneath the innocuous appearance of a plastic toy, they hide an evil witch.

Here's how. Place the fry under your bent knees, body back in plank position. In this position, cross the width of your pelvis using backward breaststroke strokes. I'll bet you 100 euros you'll lose your balance! Tuck the frit under your armpits, head out of the water and kick your legs to reach the other side. Is it easy? If, like me, you draw vague circles, that's good enough. In general, the fry —and this is its genius and mischief— slides under your arms, knees and wherever you try to wedge it, before bouncing back sarcastically a metre further.

Better still, with the frit under your abdomen, cross the width of the pool by crawling with your arms, legs straight. In no time at all, you're sinking. Forward, backward, like a Culbuto, I strain, drink the cup, recover, sink again. The instructor looks indulgent. "At your own pace, ma'am, at your own pace. We don't force you here. It's all gentle!"

In the changing room, under the shower, my girlfriend smiles: "Wasn't that too hard?"

Our coaches are right. Aquagym is both age-appropriate and demanding. Because, you see, to age well, it's all about the challenge. In fact, that's the title of the editorial in my mutual's bulletin no. 45: "De l'importance de se lancer des défis" ("The importance of setting yourself challenges"). And it goes on to sing the refrain: "Moving around when you don't feel like it, travelling when staying at home is a comfortable but worrying temptation [...] are all challenges to be overcome." You read that right: temptation. Let's not give in to temptation, as we were taught in the catechism. We need to understand both the moral and the hygienic side of things, because these days, it's all one and the same. Scientific, too. On the Web, I discover that "the goal of burning a thousand calories a week is realistic for all of us, which means seven thirty-minute walks or seven twenty-minute jogs". The accounting of souls, as it were. In the same vein, I learn that people who take part in sport gain eight years of life in good shape compared to those who are sedentary, and that regular physical activity reduces our risk of dying from heart disease by 35% to 40%. More precise, you die!

Chapter XII
A Little Lesson in Psychology

I've been "in analysis" for ten years. A decade of exploring the depths, backgrounds and double bottoms of my unconscious, from the way I used to suck my thumb, to the cries I used to make during sex. It's far from a record. I have friends who have been at it for fifteen, twenty years and more. It's become a way of life.

I owe a lot to my therapist. Thanks to her, or rather, thanks to the "work" I've "done" with her support, I've stopped drinking too much alcohol (more or less), given up having one-night stands (with a few exceptions) and no longer burst into flames at the first sign of provocation (unless it comes from my mother). I accept that my daughter is not a first star at the Opéra, but a member of the amateur ballet corps at my local conservatory. I no longer consider it a pis-aller that my eldest son is a computer scientist on fixed-term contract, even though I'd dreamed of him as an engineer, and the youngest a physio-therapist when my imagination had propelled him to the top of the medical world.

I've "become myself" and "found my place in the generational order". So why continue?

I asked myself this question last Wednesday, stuck in traffic (because my appointment is ALWAYS at 6 p.m., in the middle of rush hour).

Over the past few weeks, I've noticed that the sessions are no longer focused on "the little girl inside me". The focus is shifting. The words *"letting go"*, *"serenity"*, *"indulgence"*, *"wisdom"*, peppered the lady's discreet comments. This vocabulary smells bad. It has the rancid odor of a senior citizens' club, the saltpetre-laden smell of a sacristy and a hint of Zen boudoir.

In short, despite the analyst's language skills, his speech is easy to decode: "Settle your affairs, put your conscience at rest, prepare for the final end."

My analysis turns into a propaedeutic of death. Here's at least one who's tackling this taboo (in addition to insurance, as we'll see). I'm grateful, of course, but isn't it a bit early?

Too early or too late, I think. Because I think about it often and without panic. Is it because I don't believe in heaven? I was just about to give up when I inventoried our coaches' merchandise of wisdom.

Our psycho-coaches don't urge us to analyze - psychoanalytically, that is. It's a general opinion on their part, with no direct connection to our age group. They judge outdated "theories" such as Freudianism in particular, and Jungianism to a lesser extent, with tolerance and an amused sense of humor. They prefer short, behaviorist therapies. It's the zeitgeist. I'm almost tempted to persevere with my analysis in the spirit of contradiction. But that's not the only reason. Even if I'm a bit ridiculous, or old-fashioned, I'm not lacking in inner demons, even at my age. As the old-fashioned Sigmund so rightly wrote, "the unconscious has no age". I have no use for two-bit wisdom, in the style of "five lessons for aging well". In psychology, as in jewelry, there's such a thing as fake. I prefer the authentic.

Chapter XIII
Back to School

I stopped in front of a poster announcing the resumption of lectures at the "inter-âge" university for the elderly. It's called "inter-age" so that no one thinks that seniors are discriminated against.

Your culture is going down the drain," the poster reproaches me, "in a short while, you'll be out of touch, only able to recite the first three lines of the *Cid* monologue, the beginning of a Virgil eglogue and half a Ronsard sonnet. You won't even know the capitals of the world, which change all the time. Your grandchildren will laugh: "It's okay, Grandma, you can Google it."

I leave immediately to get the program from the town hall. The list is mind-boggling! It ranges from "Bombyx of the mulberry tree", to "Splendors of the last maharajas", "The art of building a yurt", "Diocletian and the decline of Rome", "Dietary prohibitions in the Koran, the Bible and the Torah", "Medieval illumination in Burgundy on the eve of the Renaissance", and "Painters' repentance revealed by infrared". All that in the first semester alone. Let's calm down. I know nothing about the latest maharajas, except that they've turned their palaces into luxury guesthouses. Diocletian issued an edict granting

Roman citizenship to all inhabitants of the Empire. Marine Le Pen wouldn't approve. The yurt is a kind of tent whose frame nomads assemble in three clicks, before covering it with skins. They also have a smoke-extraction system. It's clever, but it doesn't tell me why this habitat is so fashionable in the Ardèche. About the bombyx, I don't know a thing about it. It's the scientific name for the silkworm. When I was at elementary school in Montélimar, at a time when sericulture dominated the local economy, the natural science teachers had us raise these greedy worms in crates full of mulberry leaves, which they devoured at breakneck speed.

That doesn't mean I've made any progress. It's hard to go back to school when you're not sure! That's what I told my kids when they couldn't decide which college to go to: "Boy, you're going to be 22, it's about time you knew what you wanted to do!"

I'm signing up for "Splendors of the Last Maharajahs". Perhaps this subject will open a window on India, a country I've never understood anything about, despite the backpackers' tales of '68 and the years that followed.

The following Tuesday, at 4 p.m., the students crowded into the town hall's multi-purpose room. A few gentlemen. Mostly women, wrinkled and tense, but with a keen eye and an alert pen. The lecturer mumbles a "good morning", then plants himself beside his computer and sends the first photo, a carved wooden decoration. "You see here the work done in the palaces of the maharajas of Rajasthan between 1880 and 1920 to decorate balconies and roof ledges. These motifs, often erotic [*zoom*], were taken up by the first English settlers, who substituted botanical or animal themes, such as palm leaves [*zoom*] or monkeys [*zoom*]. The same motifs adorn bedheads, studded chests and armchairs. They are not unrelated to the age-old art of carpets [*click*]. I've started with the palaces of Jaipur and the surrounding area because the decorations of this region have had influences far beyond India, for example in East Africa, where they blend with Moorish motifs [*click*]. However, it cannot be asserted peremptorily, as Prof. Simon of the University of Toulouse II does, that..."

The end of the conference wakes me up. Good nap. Martine accosts me.

- Wow! This guy's got a lot of moves.

- Didn't you find it a bit specialized, lacking in context?

- Not at all. At our age, we've gone beyond the basics.

If she says so.

From now on, I'm boycotting the university for old people, which has earned me the wrath of the deputy mayor in charge of culture.

In any case, this university is a new iteration of the well-known refrain: "It all starts at 60." Come on, old people! Let's start all over again. Let's erase everything and start again, let's go back to basics, let's get down to business for real, this time we've got the time, and let's get cracking...

If only that were true, we could subscribe to it. Taking up piano, Spanish or history may appeal, and rightly so. But these "universities" (I'm talking about the ones whose programs I've read) are just the opposite: an unconstructed series of lectures on cutting-edge subjects, too cutting-edge, with speakers who are specialists, also cutting-edge, ultra-specialized, retired like us, who rehash their theses, Professors Tournesol who find an audience for their inventions, vacationers who present their travel photos. Take it all, make a batch and call it "culture". Culture in crumbs, to paraphrase sociologist Georges Friedmann's book on work in crumbs.

While we're at it, it's best to enroll in a real university. Seniors have their place there alongside the younger ones.

Chapter XIV
Sex Worldwide

If there's one activity for which our coaches (I realize I've forgotten the sexologists, urologists and gynecologists on my list) give us carte blanche, it's sex. As much as they give us a hard time about alcohol, tobacco or big food, they don't give us a hard time about sex. Better still, they encourage us to have sex. At our age, sex has nothing but virtues. It makes your skin beautiful, eliminates stress and keeps your body in good working order. It's almost as if those who don't have sex have bought themselves a ticket to the cemetery. Our assent is taken for granted. It would be nice to see the 68 generation object to this, the generation that revolted to throw its bonnet over the windmills!

Andrée received an invitation to the Rotary Club ball at the 19th town hall. There she discovered the pot aux roses. An armada of ladies our age, provocatively dressed in sheer blouses, short skirts, fishnet stockings and technicolor make-up, were shopping for guys. "You should have seen them, they were flirting all over the place!"

Les barbons, Andrée continued, were also in full swing, dressed to the nines in pointy shoes, zazzy suits and red clutches. In a way, the simplicity of the show, if not in the way it was staged, then at least in the way it was intended, was quite invigorating. It's like a tea dance. You know why you're there.

There are less flashy occasions, as I experienced in the sauna at the Boulogne swimming pool. One afternoon, I found myself alone in the cabin with a black man, as handsome as a colonial engraving. The Masai type, sleek, muscular, haughty, nonchalant, hip supple, calf sculpted, pectorals to the point (I sometimes meet blacks —sorry, men of color— in this sauna, because there are so many of them in the adjoining weight room). I look furtively at this prodigy worthy of a pagan pantheon, sheathed in my slimming black swimsuit, maintaining the discreet posture befitting a lady of a certain age. The man calls out to me:

- I bet you're the dean of the pool.

I almost fall off my seat. He continues, in a voice as mischievous as it is velvety.

- But watch out! I think that for your age, you're very well preserved. You've got the complexion of a peach, the body of a queen and firm breasts. Ah yes, beautiful woman, beautiful woman!

- After calling me the dean of the pool? Are you kidding me?

- Ah, but I'm serious, very serious. Age has nothing to do with it. You know, beautiful women, they're beautiful, period.

An angel passes. I hazard:

- I was still prettier at 30.

- Madame, don't say that. A lot of men would like to spend the night with a woman like you. Such beautiful skin! So soft, just looking at it! If you like, I'll take you to a restaurant, very kindly. On a Tuesday, if you like, I come here on Tuesdays. Wouldn't you like to go out with a handsome black man like me?

I'm dying for it, you bet! Sitting in the hot steam, two inches from his thigh, I smell his scent, see the sweat beading on his ebony skin. I deflect to hide my confusion.

- What do you do? I mean outside the pool.

He gives me a stunning smile.

- You mean me? I don't do anything. What's the point of working out? I come here to work out. I want to have a nice body so I can seduce women like you. If you like, I'm a gigolo. But no offense! I don't pluck rich women. If a beautiful lady like you invites me to a restaurant, that's enough. After that, there's no obligation, it's up to you.

I smiled. I wanted to say "yes". I've never known a Black man, biblically speaking. Alas. I heard myself say: "Already 5:30! I'm leaving you now. Excuse me, I'm dreading the traffic jam."

I put on my flip-flops and took off. What happened the following Tuesday? You guessed it.

When I told this story to Andrée, who wasn't too keen on Rotary's guinche, she assured me that she would have done the same. She would have felt uncomfortable being hit on by a gigolo, even if he was —on the face of it— an honest variant of the prototype.

In short, we're beggars can't be choosers. The mention of "cougars", those mature women from the *celebrity world* who seduce men much younger than themselves —Madonna, Susan Sarandon, Demi Moore and others— shocks me. The feline that has given these ladies their nom de guerre strikes me as a misplaced totem, fit for a depraved jet-set.

In our circles, moreover, gigolos are not legion. In this field, as in many others, globalization is the key. The national gigolo is too expensive, even on the black market, whereas for 450 euros a week, including flights, and adding a few pennies in remuneration, we can "afford" a man at the height of his virility in an exotic paradise. We sometimes suspect that our sisters' cultural journeys have an ulterior motive. Apparently, we even beat the men of our country at this game... Our destinations are numerous, if I am to believe an article in *Le Monde diplomatique*, which lists, in addition to Dominica: Haiti, Jamaica, Cuba, India and the small state of Goa, not to mention Turkey, Morocco, Tunisia and Egypt, which have already been frequented by horny grannies for many years.

Wealthy tourists will enjoy the charms of the internationally renowned gigolos of Bali, Sumatra and Sulawesi. For those of modest means, the rades of Saly, the mecca of Senegalese tourism, are overflowing with unemployed young people eager for the three Vs: visa, car and villa. In The Gambia, good addresses are no longer a secret. The Senegambia district of Banjul is an open brothel. You can find a male to your liking in bars, gyms or simply on the beaches, where beach boys sell their peckers. In this country, I read with dismay on the Internet, women represent 20% of sex tourists. One of the reasons for the success of the white woman with gigolo over the white man on holiday is that the old white woman can't have children. Local fiancées see in the trade of their promised one a way to build up their household.

Men of my generation have been using this outlet for ages to appease the appetites they claim their wives can no longer satisfy. Their desires lead them to Southeast Asia, Central America and above all Madagascar. Their Gambia is the island of Nosy Be, whose young women are said to appreciate the *vasahas* (Westerners in the local language). But our friends, ex-husbands, husbands and companions are off to Morocco, Tunisia, Dominica and Senegal, just like us. Until Madame meets Monsieur one evening in some Saly bistro...

Far from being a concession to May 68, isn't the craze for sex a way of reconciling old couples?

Chapter XV
The Linchpins:
"The Strength Is in You."

We are the "pivot generation". Let's open the *Larousse*.

"Pivot: Bearing with a vertical axis designed to support a vertical load;

Base, essential support on which everything rests, axis, keystone around which everything is organized."

So it's the figurative sense that's important, even if the word "*load*" has its own relevance.

In its current meaning, the expression means that we are the intermediate generation that provides services to our parents and children.

Our coaches are familiar with this sociological reality.

They work hard to help us be efficient pivots. It's quite an acrobatic feat to age well and be "good" pivots at the same time. The axis has to be solid. It's a difficult exercise. For me, anyway. What worries me most is the side of the axis turned towards my ancestors, in this case my mother (my father is dead), of whom I am the only daughter. With my mother, I'm a "carer", as the staff at the nursing home where I managed to find her a place after an exhausting search put it.

This home, belonging to a large specialist group, "involves caregivers in the establishment's project". It's all about being willing to visit often, to be kind to the housekeepers, to smile at the nurses, even if they're dragons in white coats, and not to overdo it with the "overworked" management.

Good. I respect the instructions. Just about. The other day, in the dining room, someone came up to me and told me I was too loud. "My mother is deaf," I objected. "Madam, you're not the only one who's deaf." What could I say?

Fortunately, I'm very popular here. Because of my dog. When I arrive with Rac at exactly noon, a shiver runs through the living room as the old folks wait to enter the dining room, hurrying towards the two still-closed doors as if they were the gates to heaven. Rac's arrival creates a timely diversion, and a bit of a mess too, as some of the residents shift the axis of their wheelchairs to look in her direction. The exclamations fly: "Oh the pretty little dog, what's his name?" Those who still have a memory: "Rac, this is Rac, this is Rac..."

Once we're seated at the table, my mother is not happy, because after a quick kiss, I do a real lap of honor with the dog, going to greet Mrs. de Roche and her fine pearl necklace, Dédé le fou (who suddenly lets out inarticulate cries), Mr. Fabre who used to work at the cartoucherie aux "acides bouillantes" and Mrs. Juste who is 101 years old and has a blank stare, except when I take Rac in my arms and bring him close to her face.

I recently learned that, like Molière's Monsieur Jourdain, I was writing prose without knowing it. This is organized in some old people's institutions under the name of zootherapy. In short, I "do" volunteer work. My coach (my guardian angel, my conscience) must be happy!

I must admit I'm a better fulcrum for the residents in general than for my mother in particular. My mother weighs me down. She has a form of delirium, Alzheimer's, which seems to have been concocted on purpose to make me grumble. She "forgets" that I take the TGV every fortnight to come and see her. She "doesn't know" that I bought her a Marcelle Griffon fine white knitted sweater, close-fitting and solid (after having her try on three, which she rejected) and claims that it was "stolen" from her, even though it's in the lingerie department. It's incredible the geography of memory lapses, a real labyrinth...

In short, I don't always keep my cool. Like many of my friends, who are also "helpers" to a mother with whom connivance has turned to hostility.

Every time I visit, I see how accurate the statistic is that there are far more female carers than male carers. I often chat with Mrs. Deroche's daughter, who's having lunch at the next table. "There are four of us, three boys and me. We all live in the area. My brothers come once or twice a year, I'm here every week." Banal, very banal...

When it comes to offspring, women also rule the roost. Grandmothers are in the front line when it comes to looking after grandchildren. You may say that if the grandmother is married, the grandfather is "impacted" (if you accept this neologism). It's not uncommon, however, for granny to be at the school gate with a snack more often than granddad. Not to mention the fact that most grannies live alone, so... It follows from this indisputable fact that, in addition to traveling, volunteering, aquagyming and choral singing, sexas grannies are also grandmothers. Real athletes, marathon runners, we are.

Well, not me. I don't have any grandchildren yet. That's not surprising for a woman in her sixties, because, as you know, today's young people are having their children "later" and "later", due to the fact that they're getting married "later", all of which is more or less linked to the difficulties they're encountering on the job market. As a result, our "axis" supports the "vertical" force of maintaining and housing our children as young adults.

Here again, I'm speaking in general terms, because I'm not a very solid person. With my 2,400 euro pension, I can't afford a studio apartment for my kids! Fortunately, they've found cheap rents (for flats in Paris) and one of them has even bought his own bungalow. I'm content to modestly maintain the country house in the certainty that it's a "pivotal" place, so to speak.

Chapter XVI
The ABCs of Volunteering

At the supermarket entrance, a young man in black pants and a green T-shirt slips me a leaflet. The leaflet calls on customers to take part in the Food Bank's collection drive "by buying basic necessities such as pasta, rice, cookies or canned goods". I oblige.

My pack of spaghetti, my tinned food and my cookies will take to the sea, crossing deserts and the borders of countries on fire, to comfort my destitute fellow human beings, left to murder, pillage, hostage-taking, despotism and ethnic rivalries, I say to myself, satisfied with a job well done.

At checkout n°4, I come face to face with a woman about my age, pudgy in green overalls and a black T-shirt. I hand her my alms. This woman reminds me of someone. Oh yes, it's a lady who used to come to the gym last year! She offered to collect donations with me. Why not, I thought, if it's for a good cause. Some of my retired friends are volunteers. For them, it's a way of making themselves useful, keeping fit and having a social life.

The government is encouraging this generous activity, which can only be a "win-win" situation. At a time when the 2010 reform is asking salaried employees to work longer, it's only fair that retirees should give a few hours of their time to a group of volunteers! He owes it to the society that has pampered him so. In return, he'll receive notoriety (in the good sense of the word) for his concern for the public good. According to the National Plan for Ageing Well (PNBV), every civil servant who leaves his or her job "will be given a passport to an active retirement, encouraging his or her commitment to volunteering".

Even if I'm not a member of the cohort of public servants, there's something here to appeal to the citizen in all of us. The weekly *Notre Temps* and its cousin *Pleine Vie*, which are aimed at our "target age", do not fail to encourage us to practice what, not so long ago, were called "good works". There's not an advice book that doesn't sing the praises of such a rewarding and useful activity. It's all the more ingenious in that many of our grandfather-boomers are sensitive when it comes to generosity. They learned their ABCs in the scouts, or collected for Secours Populaire. Later, they campaigned for the cause of the Third World. In '68, they defended the working class. Others (or the same ones) feel that they have lived well and can give a little of what they have received. Clearly, Martine is one of them.

Drawn back by a guilty conscience, I retrace my steps. I get a better look at the scene. At each cash register, silhouettes in green and black hurry past. Volunteer no. 1 receives the arrivals, Volunteer no. 2 arranges the donations in a hurry, so that an employee, who places them on a pallet, can keep up the pace. The girl wears a peaked cap that reads "OAM partner".

You could say it's assembly line work. The activity of the green and black men reproduces the mechanics of the factory and the routine of the office. On their concentrated faces, I read serious-ness and competence. Not a smile. No time! Sometimes a brief "thank you".

I reread the prospectus. It's written according to the rules of effective communication. A title, a color code, a single message, a practical way to act. The vocabulary? "Efficiency... performance... speed... traceability..." The words of the company, the words of our managers!

I try to picture silver containers, hurled from a helicopter door, falling from the sky like manna from the desert. It's no use. All I can conjure up (as I've seen so often on TV) is a pack of villagers snatching up our gifts, while soldiers try to maintain some semblance of order.

Martine is mired in *charity business*. I wouldn't go begging with her.

Yes, you'll agree, but there are thousands of small associations and groups where you can devote yourself. I have nothing against that. I'm a member of a read-aloud association. When it organizes its modest annual festival, I carry chairs and benches and cook a pizza. So am I a volunteer? I wouldn't presume to call myself one...

What worries me is the constant chorus of our gurus in favor of this activity. I did indeed say "activity", just as we say "workforce". Well, well... *Bénévolat* means a "good" will, a "free" action. In this case, free labor. As my regional daily writes on page 5 of a village boules competition: "Nothing would have been possible without the hard work of the dozens of volunteers who made the competition such a success" and, on page 6, of the Alumni lottery: "Nothing would have been possible without the hard work of the volunteers, etc."

It's very useful, this free work in times when subsidies to associations are scarce! That's fine, if the ants are happy. They're not as numerous as you'd imagine, in fact: an Insee survey on the social life of 55 to 64 year-olds puts associative life at the bottom of the pile, at 36.9%. Voting wins the day (81% and 83%), followed by manual activities (DIY, gardening) and artistic pursuits, then cultural outings (64.1%), family gatherings (58.7%) and meetings with friends (47.6%).

I conclude that our generation is not excessively inclined towards volunteering. Should we see this as a form of resistance to the insistent antiphon we're being fed? I'm probably talking too much about numbers. But I am concerned by this obsession with volunteering that we hear from all sides. By combining the flute "béné-voles, béné-voles" with the bass drum RE-TRAI-TE AC-TI-VE, RE-TRAI-TE AC-TI-VE, we play a tune whose refrain is that man, in the final analysis, is nothing but a producer.

This mutilation is nothing new, of course. A misguided conception of Marxism has led to it. But I'm talking about our liberal, democratic societies. The humanist writer Susan Sontag, who died in 2004, remarked: "The valorization of the elderly serves a society whose idols are ever-increasing industrial production and the limitless cannibalization of nature."

Behind the injunction to be "active" lies the refusal to conceive of man in his inner, contemplative dimension, the utilitarian vision of a life in which every moment must have a "return".

"Unfair! Partial!" our mentors will protest. We also recommend hobbies, reading, board games, choral singing, practicing an art —in short, fun and creative activities.

Duly noted.

But this permission should be exercised more throughout life. The latter is increasingly invaded, framed, undermined and eaten away by work. Not only because of its legal duration, but also because of the mental clutter, the notorious stress linked to increasingly intrusive management, with brain-formatting courses, laptops, smartphones, GPS and other tablets invading the private sphere. The "good life" is postponed until retirement. Canadian sociologist Bernard Arcand points out that this is an aberrant break. He denounces the promise of the only "real vacation" at age 65: "To succeed in extracting as much work as possible from each day, it was essential to tolerate only work, and to push most of the behavior of any normal human being elsewhere. It was essential to invent the third age."

Am I exaggerating? See how long we've been using the term *"third age"* instead of *"old age"*, and we'll talk about it again.

Chapter XVII
Françoise's Happy Summers

Françoise, a friend from university, spends the winter in Paris and the summer in the same commune as me. I bump into her at the market. She excitedly exclaims:

- What a joy to meet you! These Provence markets are irresistible. The colors, the smells...

- Did you just get here?

- It's been a week, but it feels like a century. I don't touch the ground. And I thought I'd take it easy when I retired.

She shakes the curls of her dramatically oxygenated perm.

- There's nothing stopping you!

- You've got some good ones! Eight friends visiting at noon; tomorrow, arrival of the children and their smala; in the evening, concert at the *Temple*. Negro spirituals. Want to come along?

- That is, uh, I prefer the classic.

- Another time, then. Jean-Claude claims his wife is a tornado. Isn't that exciting, after thirty years of marriage?

- I'm divorced, so...

- I forgot, you wore out two of them (*laughs*). And lovers, naughty, they do exist, don't they?

- Precisely...

- Whatever! I'd like to be alone sometimes too. But I'm *full*. On Monday, I'm hosting Senegalese musicians for the festival, on Tuesday I'm manning the stand for the Alzheimer's League, and then I have to fit in the mayor's potluck. O-BLI-GA-TOI-RE. The town has voted a subsidy for the Trèfles association, of which Jean-Claude is president. Do you have your card?

- I don't play bridge.

- At your age! And what about your neurons? I bet you'd rather show your face at Claude Rambert's opening.

- In other words...

- I do half and half. I go to the mayor's party with Jean-Claude and send the kids to the vernissage. Well, we're chatting now, but I've got this lunch to prepare. At 5pm, I'm off to the choir. It's a unique moment of relaxation and self-reflection. I'm completely empty. Isn't our retirement a time to let go?

- You said it. (*Smile.*)

- How are you doing?

- Yes, I walk, I write.

- Is that all? Be careful, you'll get old.

- Writing requires energy.

- It's obvious, darling. I haven't read your latest book, but don't worry, it's on my shelves.

And there she goes again, twirling, with her straw hat and her village costume, which she finds just right.

I sigh. What is it that makes her do so much? She and many others, men and women alike, all tell me they have ministers' agendas, activities to spare, "I'm leaving at the interval because I'm on to another concert", "I'm just saying hello because I'm expected", "I'd really like to come, but we're busy right now"... At 40, I understand —and even then!— But at 60, 65 or beyond?

Vitality, enthusiasm intact? Perhaps. This way, at our age, of being nowhere and everywhere, of taking off as soon as we land, makes me dizzy. I can't get it out of my head that this is a form of headlong rush, a chase with old age, a vain race against time, against death (*watch* and *death*, four letters in common). Wouldn't common sense dictate that we change tempo?

In *Esprit* magazine, Christian Pelluchon shares my astonishment: "The fact of having a long life behind us should lead us to relativize social pressure and even any image of success and glory in favor of the enjoyment of the present." Talk about gold, this Pelluchon! Pelluchon goes on to attack "a stereotypical vision of happiness that echoes the clichés conveyed by the market and the race for competitiveness". That's right. The sacrosanct religion of performance imposes its magisterium on the elderly, just as the illusion that activity is synonymous with health and youth is rampant. Pascal —Blaise— put it so well! Thought 146: "Man is obviously made to think. It's his dignity and his profession. And all his duty is to think properly [...] But what does the world think about? Dancing, playing the lute, singing, making verses, chasing rings, fighting, making themselves king, without thinking about what it is to be a king and what it is to be a man."

I like the image of little old people basking in the sun on a bench, a behavior that Françoise certainly ignores —even if there were a bench in her garden.

Chapter XVIII
Globetrotters

Nathalie and Alain have invited me to dinner with a few friends our age. As we attack the asparagus puff pastry, Annie spills her glass of water. The conversation is cut short. The clumsy (?) one seizes the opportunity.

"Excuse me. You see, I've just come back from Canada. I'm still recovering from the jette lague."

Pronounced with a Toulouse accent, *jet lag is* not lacking in picturesqueness. Let's move on. Everyone's entitled to an accent. Don't Canadians have one?

And then there's the talk of Canada, the deterioration (or not?) of the French-speaking community in Quebec, Ottawa's selective immigration policy —a somewhat *touchy* subject, which the hostess deftly veers towards the "immense virgin expanses of the North", small ports on the ice floes, sleigh rides, seals and albatrosses.

As in a game of "word ball", *snow* allows Alain's colleague Michel to recount how he went skiing with his wife, Justine, in Aspen last winter.

- We used to be loyal to Les Deux Alpes. But it's no longer tenable! The slopes are invaded by children from the 9-3 district on snow classes. Black on white is nice, but it's not too much. I'm joking, of course, hi, hi, hi. In North America, the resorts are quiet, the people well-behaved, including, incidentally, people of color.

Amérique ricochets off the forehead of Henri, in his seventies, who has booked a stay at a thalassotherapy resort in Florida.

- If your cardiologist allows it," corrects his wife. At your age, darling, who knows what tomorrow will bring?

Tomorrow bounces off Annie's cortex. She announces that after Canada, she will "do" Cambodia.

- All my friends advise me to "do" Cambodia now, because it's not yet too badly damaged by tourism. It's urgent. I hear that the crowds at Angkor are worse than at Versailles.

Justine was startled.

- Have you thought about landmines?

- Of course you can! But, according to Handicap International, the authorities have cleared historic sites of mines. Accidents only affect the local population. We're not going to pay for the crimes of the Khmer Rouge! These countries are broke, you understand. So our foreign currency is a godsend for them. At the risk of tourist overload.

Nathalie jumped.

- You're exaggerating! Tour operators have understood that people want to get off the beaten track. Granted, Fram or Go Voyages are a bunch of rednecks. But I know some very good organizers who listen and come up with innovative concepts.

Annie concedes that a "new way of traveling" is "emerging". One example is ethical travel. Whereupon Justine and Michel recount how they "did" Senegal with an NGO. They helped dig a well. They are preparing to "do" Madagascar Madagascar as part of a campaign against deforestation.

It's as if they had a list. A list of countries to "do", because the time has come to "do" travel, to "do" entire continents. Jacques Brel's song keeps running through my head: *Les Flamandes dansent dans le pré, because it's time to show off...* Travel makes for old age. They occupy time. Time that is counted by the Fates sitting at the back of the living room, in a dark corner, spinning, spinning, spinning...

Each getaway is like a line crossed off the list. Zucchinis, fruit, cheese, trout, ribs," scribbled the housewife. The planetary catalog reads: Seychelles, Thailand, Sweden, Japan and more, if still alive.

My goodness! They're going to ask me about my trip to Argentina. Oh dear, I've been there, in the capital at least, then I took a bus to Iguazú Falls through the Esteros del Iberá, the "land of shining waters" in Indian. That's all there is to it. They'll think it's pathetic. You haven't done Ushuaïa? Or the Atacama Desert? Or Bariloche? What do you want, I don't like flying over, rushing past, taking three photos and then leaving.

They're eating their salad. Hopefully, they'll forget me. Globetrotters like Annie, Michel and Justine have eaten so many palms, guava trees, breadfruit trees and pineapple plants that they have to regurgitate them, again and again, at friends' houses so that they can leave with their stomachs and minds free to prepare to "do" new countries.

Graze, graze, graze!

Let's finish this salad and move on to the cream pie, quickly, quickly.

Phew! I drink my coffee and go to the bathroom. My head is spinning. "I apologize. Slight discomfort. I'll be on my way. Thank you for a delightful evening."

It's crazy, this travel mania. As soon as people have three pennies (small pensioners aren't members of the clan), they're off gallivanting around the world. It's like they've got "compulsory travel" written on their foreheads. It would be a narrow-minded departure from the rule not to tarmac upon tarmac. I completely understand the desire to get to know other peoples and broaden one's ideas through contact with other ways of life. But is that a reason to run around the planet like restless fish? I'm talking about fish because, in the final analysis, the world is just one big jar.

Wouldn't it be wiser to take only selected trips and stay put for a while? I'm reminded of Pascal's famous thought 139 (him again): "I've discovered that all the misfortune of men comes from one thing, which is not knowing how to rest in a room." Don't you mean a "retreat"?

Chapter XIX
Revival

Recently, I was invited by my pension fund, Audiens (which covers former employees of the press, books, communications and entertainment industries) to take part in courses on ageing well run by Marie de Hennezel. And I went to a conference in Paris where these courses were presented.

Frankly, we're not being laughed at, because this charming woman is a benchmark in the field of aging well and support for the dying. Her book *La Mort intime (Intimate Death)* was prefaced by François Mitterrand, and *Nous ne nous sommes pas dit au revoir (We didn't say goodbye),* another of her bestsellers, propelled her to the position of rapporteur to the then Minister of Health, Jean-François Mattei, and her conclusions largely inspired the Leonetti law on the end of life.

Five years ago, she published *La chaleur du cœur empêche nos corps de rouiller (The Warmth of the Heart Prevents our Bodies from Rusting).* It was this book that inspired the National Plan for Ageing Well. The seminars led by Mrs. de Hennezel last five days, are interactive, says the moderator, and feature numerous practical exercises.

It's undoubtedly a very good course. Mrs. de Hennezel's sphere of influence forbids her, like that brave Mr. Vinot (whom I pin in the "Our coaches" chapter), to utter platitudes. She leaves it to the servants to take care of the housekeeping, such as walking or water aerobics. As she said at the conference, "I'm wondering about the spiritual meaning, in the broadest sense" of old age.

We must always be wary of the spiritual "in the broad sense". It is often spiritual in the strict, even narrow sense. The crucial question, according to Mrs. de Hennezel, when we reach the age of 60, is: "How can we be a source of joy for others? Yes, a "source" of joy, because what is old age, eh, if not "a spiritual adventure" (bis)? And to quote Saint Paul: "While our outward man is going to ruin, our inward man is being renewed day by day." Don't get it? Take a detour into etymology: in Hebrew, *gil* means both "to be old" and "to be drunk with joy". Want to know more? A little ethnology: in Amerindian tradition, death is a bird perched on the left shoulder. Let's ask ourselves, with Jacqueline de Romilly," suggested Mrs. de Hennezel in this talk, "whether the propensity to remember old things, which increases with age, is not in fact an "experience of eternity". For a moment, I thought I was listening to a priest's, rabbi's or pastor's homily, but I also had some for myself, a miscreant, on the grounds that "even" Stéphane Hessel, who "calls himself" an atheist (believers "are" believers, atheists "call themselves" atheists) speaks of the inner joy that animates his 90-year-old frame. Chantons alléluia, de 60 à 100 ans, chantons, mes frères!

Chapter XX
Take off Those Jeans

My current favorite book is about a former hippie who has become a best-selling author. The gentrified man values his girlfriend's opinion. Here he is, in the garden, reading aloud to her from the novel in progress, while she trims a hedge, perched on a ladder, wearing blue jeans.

So the husband addresses his wife's buttocks, a point of view that prompts a cry from the heart: "After 50, a woman should never wear jeans again." What a macho guy he is. Ah, they've changed a lot since Woodstock, those flower men!

However, I read in the autumn issue of *Pleine Vie* that jeans worn with a "sport-chic" jacket guarantee a silhouette that's "both youthful and elegant". I've deduced that this fabric is still appropriate for us sexas.

Investigating at Damart, I realized that jeans for old ladies aren't real jeans, but elasticated pants with ease pleats, cut from a fabric that looks like denim.

I often wear them —real ones— because it saves me from wearing out my "nice pants", the ones for dressy occasions. In the morning, everything prompts me to put on jeans: sweeping the yard, walking the dog, cleaning the cellar, vacuuming. No husband to comment on my figure. As for the dog, he sees everything in gray.

This remark, coming from a good writer, still bothered me. I plant myself in front of my mirror.

Objectively. Face, profile. Patatras! My jeans pocket under the buttocks, twist at the knees, godille on the calves, before collapsing to the ground. This snob is right.

It's not so much my jeans that are wrong as my body in them. And yet, I'm only slightly overweight, I wear a size 42 and I work out. Still... The magic of a pair of jeans worn by a young woman, these buttock-shaping, Venus-highlighting, leg-extending pants, don't stand the test of time. An intangible "minus" in tone, gait and arch is enough to produce a disproportionate effect: jeans no longer fit.

I decide to get it over with.

I've already given up the bikini, the topless, the mini-skirt and the stilettos, but without pain: the fashion was over.

Mourning the loss of jeans is an ordeal. Goodbye Vespa, flirts, boyish manners, rock'n'roll! I bury the last vestige of my yé-yé years. I'm throwing all my jeans in the garbage can.

Except for one. The one I wear to sweep the yard, walk the dog, clean the cellar and so on.

Chapter XXI
Wear Them Red and Short

At the village market, a strange feeling assails me. It's as if everyone looks the same. No, not everyone. Rather, the women. I take a closer look. I pass two middle-aged housewives. Their hair is short and reddish. The more I walk, the more I notice the profusion of shaved carrot hairs. It's unbelievable! The more I look, the more I get the impression that ALL women my age have red hair and are closely shorn.

This blush comes in many shades. It ranges from pure carrot to Venetian blond, beet red and purplish orange. Clipping can be total or partial (top of the head, parietals, nape of the neck). The rest of the hair is brushed, or even trimmed with bangs or long side locks. Amazing!

Of course, it's been a long time since grannies in the countryside abandoned the gray bun twisted at the nape of the neck or the perm enhanced with a touch of Regecolor. For some years now, medium-length hair and straight or plunging bobs have been the order of the day.

Blow-drying had supplanted perming. Colors ranged from soft to dark blonde. Even brunettes were going blonde, sometimes forgetting their eyebrows and moustache. Where on earth did this epidemic of short, red hair come from? A local hairdresser's fantasy? There are at least fifteen salons in the town, all in fierce competition with each other. Could it be that the professional association has made a secret deal with dye manufacturers to sell off unsold stock? Nonsense! Our local investigative weekly has already uncovered the scam. I guess the matrons like it that way. Is it the memory of the henna rinses of their youth? Does this aggressive color reflect a feminist stance, fifty years after 1968? Does it signify a suicidal intention to imitate the punkettes, a feminine specimen no longer in existence?

Red here, brush there. Have the Figaros fooled their customers, arguing that blood color gives a youthful glow?

Imposture! This hairstyle, to put it bluntly, is a calamity. The abrupt red and the harsh brush accentuate the features, emphasize the pockets, cast a satanic glow on the face, and erase even the most tenuous expression of tenderness. Perhaps it's a kind of totem, a tribal sign? According to Julie, who lives in a small town in Corrèze, and Sylvie, a village in Pas-de-Calais, the situation borders on epidemic. Conversely, the Parisian women with second homes have made a different choice. I suddenly realize this when I meet my friend Annie. They wear their white hair naturally, like many of the capital's grand bourgeoises. These subtleties escape me. I've stuck to a blond that's neither light nor dark, without thinking too much about the consequences for my image.

Chapter XXII
Be Beautiful Forever

Spas are all the rage. In a maze of rooms dotted with Jacuzzis and reeking of incense, reclining on bamboo beds or tatami mats, contemporary odalisques can choose between a relaxing hot stone treatment, a Californian massage or a vomit-colored mud wrap.

These "beauty areas", with their gurgling fountains and Indo-Thai-Moroccan decor, where you leave the kneading or warming bed to relax in tiny tubs known as "pools", look the same all over the world. What a bore! It's the ultimate in beauty, however, and even in the small town where I live in summer, a boutique stocked with them is a big hit.

Men are getting in on the act too. In the past, men's beauty or massage salons were the hideaway for shops dedicated to highly localized massages. This is no longer the case. Today, men go to beauty salons to get rid of dimpled skin, be waxed, coated with rejuvenating cream or relieved of dead skin, before immersing themselves in hot, warm or cold basins, just like us women (although the old-fashioned massage salons have not disappeared).

But I'm on the verge of going off-topic here, because every generation in their forties (young people don't have any money before that) frequents these avatars of the Roman baths.

What I want to talk to you about with this example is the supposed obsession with youth among people in their sixties, which is said to be reaching new heights, a paradoxical statement given that they are all supposed to be "young and beautiful". It's not just a contradiction, it's a vague reference to an alleged "zeitgeist" that leads my generation to rebel, as never before, against the stigma of old age.

Some of my friends have taken an important step. In addition to their regular visits to the spa, they've crossed the threshold of a "medicalized" institute ("attention, mé-di-cali-sé", that's serious!) to consult specialists who, "after a thorough psychological analysis", have sold them a range of very expensive techniques such as injections, aspirations, abrasions, exhurdations and so on, as science progresses by the minute. As for these gentlemen, they too have pushed open the door of the capilliculturist or the aesthetic clinic.

Looking young? But for whom, for what? For US! chorus the columnists in the women's magazines and the columnists in the men's magazines on the page. BECAUSE WE WANT IT! echo the TV screens between 7.30pm and 8pm. This first-person plural is misleading. It's not a royal *we*, an endangered grammatical usage. It's a *we* that's supposed to reflect the desire of a few suckers my age, a desire strongly stimulated by advertising and other hurriedly completed surveys, inspired above all by the desire to reassure those younger than us.

What are we instilling in these young people, in OUR CHILDREN, with no fixed job, no status, on the brink of downgrading? That they're the victims of a terrible injustice, that their parents are young and handsome (and rich), that they're clinging to prebends that bar young people from the job market. Worse, that their moms and dads will cost them dearly, dearly, if they become "dependent", because then they'll have to pay to hide them behind the walls of expensive old people's homes. A perverse discourse concocted to stir up a supposed generational conflict, when our children undoubtedly love us better than we loved our parents, blinded by their social success, or presumed success, during the Trente Glorieuses.

The guilt-ridden discourse directed at the younger generation is disturbing. They ask themselves: how can we resolve the opposition between parents/bullies and parents/loved ones?

By magic, my goodness! We parents MUST stay young, eternally young, beautiful and healthy, sexas *forever*. It's as if, thanks to gymnastic exercises, vitamins, massages, cosmetic and reconstructive surgery, we'd found the elixir of youth. Don't lose your CONSERVED (canned) youth, don't compromise your beauty, your petulant shape, your intact sexuality...

Mom, always be my beautiful mom, no wrinkles, no fat, no infirmities, you understand, mom my future depends on it, and you, papinou, keep a flat stomach, please, no paunch, no cholesterol, no stroke, please dad, don't lose your hair or else get implants.

Mom, in her size 38-40 swimsuit (42 maximum if she's blossoming), stands forever on the edge of her bourgeoise pool, all smiles, her face lifted, with just a few fine lines that her sunglasses are enough to hide. She poses for the photo, if not at the edge of her pool, at least near the tiny body of water in her suburban garden. And you, Dad, are standing next to her, tucking in your belly as you take the photo. It's easy, you've got so little belly, with all the cycling you do.

No, I'm wrong, Mom will be alone in her deckchair by the pool, but she'll still be smiling in her size 44 swimsuit (a Weight Watchers performance), and we won't see the scars from her three C-sections hidden in the pubic hair, nor those from her hip prosthesis, because she'll have artfully laid her towel over them. As for Dad, he'll be on a beach in front of coconut palms (unless it's the Aquaboulevard in Paris), smiling with all the white teeth of his dentures and tucking in his stomach to the point of asphyxiation, posing next to his charming third wife, aged 42, of whom he has two toddlers the same age as mine (damn Dad, always green!) and I'll take the photo, phew, Dad's doing damn well, I won't have to pay for his old people's home.

Don't worry dad, don't worry mom, if by any chance you're slightly overweight, there's a "retouch" option in the "photo" function of my iPad, ten kilos less in one click and I can also, at will, remove your few wrinkles, there you go, the photo's there, look, there, on the screen, how young and beautiful you are, stay that way for heaven's sake, amen.

Chapter XXIII
Die Well Insured

How nice they are, Bernard Le Coq and Anny Duperey, the heroes of the series *Une famille formidable*! How we love them, the two of them, right there on our screens, with their little worries and their big joys. The other day, I caught up with them at commercial time, before the news. Anny looks all upset.

- I dreamt you were dead!" she said to her companion.

- But no, darling, I'm very much alive," smiles the good Bernard. In any case, with funeral insurance, we can rest easy.

I'm reproducing the dialogue roughly, because I too was afraid that Bernard had left us. Whew! It was just a nightmare.

Insurers are coaches of the first order. They innovate every day to make our lives, and even our deaths, easier. First, they invented long-term care insurance, so that we can afford a home for the elderly, or medical expenses that exceed our fees. I learn that shares in Orpea, a leading player in long-term care, have jumped from 6.77 to 2 euros "on the back of solid half-year sales and optimistic forecasts".

Some of these philanthropists are masked. On the Bienvieillir. com website, the subscription form contains a question with an asterisk designating a "mandatory field": "Are you already a

Prévoir customer?" Prévoir, insurer of families and professionals, as its *base line* indicates. La Compagnie des femmes, as its name does not clearly indicate, has found it ingenious to segment the market. As "the first broker dedicated to women", it enables us to create a kitty for optical or dental expenses, the female side of which we can't afford to miss.

All it takes is one click to prepare for the sad event to come. So I click. And then I ask for the brochure, because I'm old-fashioned, I like to read on paper.

"You have to think the worst to stop thinking it," says the prospectus. "No one likes to imagine their own death. However, it only takes a few minutes and a handful of euros to protect your loved ones in the event of your death. We offer you the guaranteed death family contract. It's fantastic!"

I call the toll-free number to find out more about this miraculous solution.

A young woman gives me a short briefing. No medical questionnaire, guaranteed capital on death. She asks for my date of birth and, after a brief calculation, tells me that I'll have to pay "only" 31 euros a month for a proper funeral, on an estimated basis of 4,000 euros, including the religious ceremony.

- What about atheists?

- Withdraw around 200 euros.

- Are my children the only beneficiaries?

- The capital is paid to your legal heirs or any other person of your choice.

- Is there a ceiling on this amount?

- You are entitled to 10,000 euros and you can double this amount, i.e. 20,000 euros, net of inheritance tax.

- A kind of death, uh, life insurance?

- Not really, because it's a simple capital guarantee - there's no annuity. Please note that the money will be paid within 48 hours to your heirs, who will also benefit from our psychological assistance. What's more, if you die abroad, we take care of repatriation and, in certain destinations, the coffin.

- Still, 20,000 euros for a funeral…

- Your children are free to use this money as they wish.

- What if they don't use it to bury me?

- It's their business, but that's what it's for. It's a moral contract between you and them.

- With receipts?

- No receipts.

- Great! But how do I know what my funeral will cost?

- You'll need to get quotes from professionals. In our brochure, we only indicate the current rates. I should add that we offer to help your children analyze quotes free of charge, should they be caught unawares, because this business is a real jungle. For example, fees are higher in Paris than in the provinces.

- For me, it will be provincial, I think. Well, as far as I can anticipate… And cremation is one of my last wishes.

- Very well. Cremation is cheaper than burial.

Interesting conversation, isn't it? A monthly sum, a "handful of euros", therefore, to enable my children to do their final homework for me, if they allocate the guaranteed capital to this pious mission.

If you look at it closely, it's mainly a way of giving money away free of inheritance tax, a sort of tax niche.

Under the terms of another "product" offered by the same insurer, called Essen'Ciel, you can pass on up to 75,000 euros. Expensive funerals! Here, the lump sum is only paid out in the event of an accident, in other words, sudden death with no medical cause. The first formula is less advantageous from a tax point of view, but also covers death due to illness, albeit with a two-year waiting period. Insurance is always a bit of a headache.

- Are you saying that, if I take out a policy now and die of illness in less than two years, my children won't get the guaranteed capital?

- That's right, ma'am. They'll just be reimbursed for the contributions you've paid up to that point. That's normal, because we don't require a medical questionnaire.

- Ah yes, that's normal. But they won't be able to bury me...

- Please feel free to visit our website, dear lady. I'm delighted that this interview has helped to clarify things for you. Any further questions?

No further questions.

I can see that it's a long way from ads to lips, but that's what ads are for. Above all, I understand, as clearly as a contract written in size 8, that it's just another trick to pass on one's heritage without making our poor penniless children pay, without even forcing them to bury us decently.

It's the world turned upside down, this death that you can get rid of with a click. As if we could get rid of this "thought" ("think the worst so you don't have to think about it") that way, just like that, in five sets. A society that never looks death in the face, except to say, with the nerve of a financial coach, that we shouldn't make it a "taboo" when we entrust it to him.

Isn't death taboo when it comes to giving us a big scare with this Bernard le Coq who almost, even in his dreams, passed the gun to the left? Oh the big fear, the filthy fear that our children won't be "able" to pay us the last honors! So we shouldn't even pretend that they're laying the obolus for Charon under our tongues? On pain of "malvieillance", we'd have to deduct another contribution from our pensions (because we're rich...). And here we are, infantilizing our heirs with this "assistance in reading an estimate" and this "psychological assistance". Is it an exaggeration to speak of gall when these merchants of death dare to write (and I quote from the same leaflet): "From 30 cents a day, leave a good memory!"

It reminds me of the title of a book by Jacques Généreux: *La Dissociété.* That's really the word: we're cutting the links between generations, dissociating them. And, what's worse, under the pretext of preserving them! How can we, after all, advocate a return to some kind of "education in respect" or "values"?

(AUTO)PORTRAIT(S)

CHAPTER XXIV
INCONTINENCE

My dog peed on a canvas.

I was strolling through a village lined with art galleries in its picturesque medieval streets, as the brochure says, when the irreparable happened.

Rac is raised with a stick. I've made him a "citizen dog". I'm aware that, in our globalized world, everyone must strive to live in harmony, from donkeys to horses, wild boars to hunters, quad-bikers to hikers, skiers to surfers, and dogs to artists.

I'd wandered into the sculptor's, the jeweler's, the potter's, courteously asking permission to enter with my pet, when my eye was caught by a canvas at the entrance to a painting gallery. I forgot about my doggie, or, if you prefer, I let my doggie forget about himself.

The artist, dressed in an ample Berber tunic, comes running up: "Of course, I suspected as much, I came very close to warning you." Her blue eyes, matching the oriental fabric, stare at me with the contempt befitting an old lady.

The outraged canvas is covered with varnish. I take out a Kleenex, wipe it off and, presto, no more pee! I say triumphantly: "Don't worry, I've cleaned it up. The lady has to agree. I'm off again, my dignity regained, when —*boom*!— my foot hits a large pebble. Unbalanced, I fall. The dog barks. My elbows and knees are skinned. Passers-by raise their voices in distress: "Are you all right? Would you like a glass of water? A compress?" The diva of the paintbrush, all fury tucked away, pulls out a chair for me. Rage devours my stomach. I've gone from being an ill-bred granny to a "poor old granny". I say thank you, get up, run away, turn the corner. My eyes are full of tears. I rummage in my bag. No more Kleenex.

This is a very serious anecdote. Because I'm incontinent. Otherwise, I wouldn't have tripped over that damned stone and burst into tears.

We're talking *mezzo voce* here. Admittedly, one brand of intimate protection products has tried to break the taboo and expand its market, hitherto limited to young women. Its TV advert tells a suggestive story of a beautiful, slim woman of about my age climbing onto a camel. We see, in low angle, her bottom perched on the animal. A slim, muscular behind, a well-preserved 60-year-old behind as it should be, but, what's more, molded in impeccable beige pants. The lady, says the voice-over, is suffering from a minor bladder problem. But she preserves her secret with a thin, "absolutely invisible" towel. Wow! I've never managed to slip protection like that into my underpants. I must be putting them on wrong.

All this to tell you that at a family lunch just today, I excused myself from the intimate room, citing an emergency. We were three cousins and a cousin. In front of the cousin, I kept my mouth shut. But when he, in turn, asked for the place, our words were set free. It was a festival of laughter.

- I always stand at the end of a row at the cinema.

- I know the exact place between Grenoble and Valence where I can stop when I'm driving.

- For me, the most dramatic situation is to be in a touring coach with no toilet facilities and have to stop all the passengers.

- Well," says my cousin back at the table, "I don't do too well myself sometimes. The other day, I was taking a lady to a movie, a lady I'd been lusting after (he's a bachelor), and I cracked up in the queue. I isolated myself by a tree at full speed, but that had chilled her for the evening..."

Sioux tricks to avoid the worst are clever. In addition to sitting at the end of a row at the show, there are, in bulk: refrain from drinking twenty-four hours before any show, cinema, exhibition or other event; ask about the venue as soon as you enter, or even scout it out in advance; always carry a sweater or cloth that you can tie over your hips if the irremediable happens; carry in your bag something to change into at the first opportunity, once the misfortune has arrived; if there are no conveniences, search the terrain with your eyes, looking for a space between two cars or a welcoming cul-de-sac; finally, to avoid fatal discomfort due to overly long bladder restraint, plan an emergency stop on the freeway or road, with a plausible explanation such as "my engine's misfiring" or "I'm almost out of fuel". But this pretext presupposes driving on reserve, which redoubles the risk, so that this little infirmity could lead us to the cemetery before our time, in such a hurry.

Chapter XXV
Our Boo-boos

"Moderate osteoarthritis of the right hip," concluded the radiologist. "Moderate" is a good word for it! The pain sneaks up on me, infiltrates my hip, runs down my thigh, slides to my knee and insinuates itself all the way to my toes. It invades my brain like venom. Chemistry from hell!

When my grandmother told me that her bones made her suffer, I was incredulous. *Suffering* was the word used to describe Jesus on the cross, or the wounded in WW14. Well, without exaggeration, that's what I feel deep down in my bones.

I still go out shopping. Passers-by are playing blind. A child hits me with his scooter. No excuse. Behind me, an impatient pair of sneakers hits the back of my shoes. She overtakes me.

Stiletto heels look down on me.

I enter the baker's, hobbling along.

- For the little lady, it will be?

- Two chopsticks.

- 3.60 euros.

- I've got the account.

I do the extra to give the saleswoman time to put in a good word or give me a sympathetic smile. Empty stare.

The greengrocer plays dumb. He runs up his bill at top speed on his super calculator. He cashes in and holds out a sprig of parsley as alms. I try to lift my basket. Too bad. Do you think he'll give me a hand? He turns his head away, the bastard, and serves the next customer, while the queue looks on incensed. "Can't you see you're in the way!"

I enter the café to comfort myself. I throw myself like a sledge-hammer against the bar to keep my balance. The waiter gives me a sullen look.

"Noisette, as usual?"

I don't care about your hazelnut, I just want to settle down a bit, catch my breath, don't you get it, Dick? I don't have the guts to say that. I nod, the cup arrives, I drink, put 3.20 euros on the counter, pick up my burden and walk slowly, stopping on a bench, to the house.

After hobbling around for two years and spending an entire summer unable to leave my garden, I opted for surgery. Ah, that's positive, I assure you, I proclaim it. I walk like I used to, I run, I ride horses. A joy without a name, a rebirth. I'd be remiss if I didn't say a word, however, about my companions in the reha-bilitation department, for whom "it didn't work out". Too late, too much weight (overweight is the enemy), embolism despite wearing compression stockings, stubborn scarring. It's true that this is rare for "hips", as orthopedists call them. For knees, it's commonplace. Some patients are on their third operation, but there's no stopping medical progress, and this time will hope-fully be the right one. Be positive, because in surgery, morale is 50% of success (and don't forget the extra fees, please).

Chapter XXVI
Great Departures

On the eve of public holidays, the TV news revolves around bridges. Easter, May 1st, May 8th, Pentecost... All the provincial correspondents are on the bridge, ready to give us *live coverage* of the joys and sorrows of the bridge. A fine chestnut, a superb social topic.

Alert! The 30th is classified red! Worse, the 31st is black! Bison futé blows a wind of panic from its powerful nostrils. On the 1st, we'll have a little respite, as the blinker turns orange. But it won't last, as Météo-France predicts a hellish weekend.

The Rosny-sous-Bois HQ is transformed into a combat HQ.

A reminder of the instructions to follow in wartime: stop every two hours, hydrate babies and the elderly, don't forget dogs in the parking lot (or children, as we've seen). Respect speed limits, put on fog lights if necessary, check windshield wipers, watch tire pressure!

Curled up on my sofa, I can vaguely hear the racket of military preparations. My gaze is riveted on the pages of a novel whose characters know only the horse as a means of transport. The plot runs at breakneck speed and fires my imagination.

The insistent television noise finally makes me look up. Endless lines of cars wait at the Fleury-en-Bière toll booth. Travelers are hot. Kids are squealing. Just looking at the pictures, I can smell the diesel and the melted tar.

In the foreground, the special correspondent (a trainee at France Bleu) inserts her microphone through the open window of a Renault Espace.

- So how do you feel about your departure?

Man (driving):

- We left at five o'clock, to keep cool.

Everything's fine, we're happy.

- That's a record traffic jam, isn't it?

- Well, here at the toll, there's a bit of traffic, but it'll clear up. Plus, we've got air conditioning.

The microphone sinks to the passenger.

- And you, Madame, what do you think of this red-letter day?

- As my husband says, it's nothing but happiness.

The lady smiles. It's not every day you get to be on TV. The children wave at the interviewer.

- The kids are thrilled, aren't they, kids? comments the journalist.

A light wind rustles the branches in the garden. I begin reading Chapter V, page 116. The princess lifts her veil. The bold warrior discovers, horrified, that the lady of his thoughts is none other than his sister. Will the incest be consummated?

Fleury-en-Bière? Traffic jams? Accidents? Eight dead and four injured not far from Beaune? To hell with those slobbering snails and their ill-behaved children!

"Gnan, gnan, gnan, c'est que du bonheur", you bet!

I dive back into my book.

I don't do bridges. I'm not part of any major departure. No more on the A7 than at the Gare de Lyon in Paris, where travelers jostle each other between the fake palm trees. I'm retired, trala-lère, zonponpon la lire-lette!

I'm gloating. Ah, the poor people! Ah, the fools!

It's as if I'd forgotten that I too, not so long ago, was moving at a snail's pace in my Twingo, with my three kids, the dog on the verge of vomiting, the trunk full to bursting with luggage, the fuel gauge on "reserve"...

"Darn, I forgot Rintintin's lunchbox!" And I grumbled, in the Maurienne, in the Tarentaise, at toll booths or on improbable alternative routes. I'd queue up on the ring roads, at the ferry terminals, the never-ending queue.

Except, my friends, it's over, over, over! I travel on off-peak days, at off-peak fares, at off peak times. Sometimes I even pay less in first class than in second. With the Senior Card, this miracle is possible. Zero bridges, pulverized viaducts, scrap the big departures!

I look around. My living room is deserted. The dog is dozing. I shiver slightly. There's not much going on here, is there?

Chapter XXVII
The Vixen in the Tracksuit

The young women in my neighborhood go jogging on Saturday mornings.

Molded into satin-finish leotards, they move with a supple, fast stride. They wear ear-mounted MP3 players that calculate their heart rate, calories burned, average speed and a host of other parameters. Extravagant, isn't it? They run through the forest, deaf to birdsong. They listen to Radio Nova.

When I pass them, dressed in my fleece Adidas tracksuit, my three-stripe sneakers on my feet, exhaling with a "choo-choo, choo-choo", their eyes secrete a film as hard as ice. As if on a tiny TV screen, I read on the cornea: "What's with that vixen in the tracksuit? Does she think she's playing sports? Sport! Look at that nineties outfit, a real specimen of pre-sport humanoid."

I resume my run, grumbling at those pretentious little bitches who think they're sexy when they're just skinny. Let's say I'm jealous.

What do they care, I ask myself, if I'm wearing a pair of out-of-date jogging pants and feel like running? I rack my brains before I grasp the obvious. If I've met their icy eyes, it's because I've looked at them! Elementary, my dear Watson.

"From a certain age, you have to walk with your eyes down," my grandmother once told me. In ancient times, I interpreted.

Now I understand. Yes, eyes downcast, like the young girls in the cités where the caïds rule! Just like the title of Tahar Ben Jelloun's book! Except that here, it's the "old women" who are forbidden. Should we shave the walls, lower our eyelids and leave the high ground to these high-tech messengers?

I finish my three park laps with this disturbing observation. If I give in on the look, I'll give in on the rest. At the movies, I laugh when it's funny, sob when it's sad. My daughter nudges me. She whispers, "You're showing off, Mom." One thing leading to another, I'll be shaving the walls, becoming invisible. No way!

It's more important not to look down than to smooth your eyelids with a laser.

Chapter XXVIII
A Walk into the Past

One sunny morning, I set off for a walk along a path I've loved since childhood. It looks impressive from below, as it's set into a high cliff. In fact, after a short climb, the rock hides a comfortable path between its folds.

Conquering this trompe-l'oeil fortress gives me the delicious feeling of putting myself in danger for a laugh. I walk briskly. Rac zigzags and sniffs, nose to the ground.

Suddenly, he leaps up, howling, his fur bristling. I perked up my ears, looking for a wild boar, another dog, a rodent, an adder. Nothing. I flush out the culprit: a wire, camouflaged in the greenery, runs along both sides of the path. I put my hand on it. A jolt shakes me. So, "my" path is lined with an electric fence this year. No wonder my six-kilo dog reacted! That's when I remember absent-mindedly reading a sign, as new as the wires, at the start of the path: "Hike for beginners: duration two hours. Please stay on the trail and keep dogs on a leash". Marked trail, electric wires, leash.

Sad conclusion: no more "promenade", that word symbolizing wandering and fantasy, which carries in its three-and-a-half syllables permission to leave the trail, tumble down the slope, improvise zigzags and variants. Hiking, as the sign suggests, sounds like a long walk over difficult terrain, requiring effort and special equipment in case of an unexpected storm or gale. It's a ridiculous misnomer to refer to a walk that can't exceed four kilometers and a hundred meters above sea level. All this, I bet, so that the tourist office can display an impressive number of kilometers of "hiking". Or, who knows, so that senior citizens can boast that they "do" hiking. Good for you, eh?

Anger fills me. These wires, I want to rip them out. This sign, I want to dig it up and smash it to pieces. "Vandalism", said the staff in charge of the paths. "Endangering wildlife with a stray dog", accused the forest ranger. The irruption of new regulations in my most intimate sphere, that of my childhood, enrages me.

Invoke my memories as a little girl, when the guard calls me in, try to plead that I've been coming here for thirty years? He'll say that's no reason (in other words, unreasonable). He'll grumble (as an aside): "That old lady, she's living in the past."

In truth, I'm not unaware that "the paths are designed to make the countryside a zone of harmonious coexistence between all the players", as the mayor, who loves technocratic novlangue, puts it. But when my favorite place is attacked, I feel sad. If I were to go beyond this epidermal reaction, my anger would remain, because I also know that this obtuse discourse applies to the roads that *remain,* to the *remnants of* the rural roads that have now been erased.

I suppose that a man or woman of 30 is capable of lamenting, as I do, the decline of agriculture, the concreting of soils, the disappearance of rural dirt roads and the transformation of agricultural space into a tightly regulated recreational area. But he will be unable, like me, at 60 years of age, to distinguish the traces that have disappeared. I see them, I feel their former texture under tar or crops, their smell after rain, their dust in full sun. It's a myriad of sensations where space and time overlap, a thick book of space-time that I reread. All the more so, *a fortiori*, for the paths that remain. But I don't approve of denaturing them with absurd names or fencing them off. This so-called "preservation" is nothing more than putting them under a bell, a museification, an embalming.

When I was a little girl, I used to hear an "old man" —a man of my age today, no doubt— walking with a stick for a cane, pointing to a heap of brambles and ivy and announcing that this was his grandmother's house, I wondered if he wasn't softening his brain, until he showed me, hidden under the vegetation, the three steps of the threshold and the large stones of the entrance. So I realize how difficult it is to explain this new way of looking at things that we acquire as we get older, to younger people. They are too quick to think that we are nostalgic or that we miss the good old days. That can happen. But it's quite possible to have the gift of double vision, and still enjoy the present to the full. Perhaps we love life even more when we weave it with the past.

Sometimes I organize a treasure hunt into the past. The itinerary is made up of paths that have disappeared, but are visible thanks to the infrared of memory, like the aerial archaeologist, who can see the Roman road beneath the crops thanks to the slightly different color of the soil.

Along with a few of my smuggler friends, we took the path known as "la chèvre au piquet". It used to wind northwards through a hedge of wild pear trees, brambles and lilac, suddenly widening at the height of a small pothole where thick grass grew and a goat, tied by a chain to a stake, grazed melancholically.

Today, it has been widened and asphalted. It's easy to walk along (easier than it used to be) up to a certain point where the "top" road forks, while the underlying path is reduced to a sente, which we take. It leads to a private property. We sneak in, stepping over the small fence that runs along the bottom of the garden. We glide silently down to the stream. Here, there was (and still is, if you can see) a ford where the herds were led to drink. We cross the shallow water and climb back up the opposite slope, skirting a field that leads to a lane we can only remember. That's it, we've reached a new path that takes us back to our neighborhood.

These escapades remain secret, because it's not fashionable to talk about the past. Aging well requires us to "project" ourselves into tomorrow, into the future, to submit to the law of the stopwatch that measures our stride, to criss-cross the vast paths of a joyous and inconsistent future, devoted to leisure, entertainment and silly games like walking in a group with ski poles.

So here I am, after this mental detour, planted on the path that my 12-year-old heart adored as the privileged place of my daydreams, and which has ever since been the refuge of a slow time, stolen from the agitation of the world; to access it, now that I have "time", as they say around me, I have to resist an electric fence that confines my gestures while trying to confine my soul. Fortunately, I'm still agile.

These two wires are not landmines. I'm free to ignore this stupid sign. Resolution taken, I straddle the impediment to walking in circles and roll down the slope on my behind, shouting "yippee!!!" Smell of leaves, brush of insects, scratches of brambles, my 12 years are here, they're back! The dog overtakes me, turns around, comes back up, tongue hanging out, all happy.

A jolt to my coccyx immobilizes me. I land on hard ground, strewn with turbid puddles. My ears pop under the blast of a hellish noise. An oblong shape enters my field of vision. A motorcycle hurtles towards me. It grazes me, nearly knocks me over and splashes me.

I'm up to my nose in mud. I catch sight of another speeding car, then others. I shudder to my feet, only to come up against a sign: "Motocross, reserved area, danger".

Rac barks like a rabid dog. What if he causes an accident? Dangerous animal, to the pound! I recall him with great difficulty. I climb back up, out of breath and covered in shit. I cross the electric fence.

What do I see when I arrive, exhausted, on the path? A guy on a mountain bike! I'll show him. I drop my miniature hound against his wheel. The culprit puts his foot down. "Sir," I tell him sternly, "this is a footpath only. Didn't you read the sign down there?"

Chapter XXIX
Deadly Spring

The first snowdrops move me to tears. Forsythia dazzles me, lilac intoxicates me, wisteria bewitches me.

This year, however, I feel strange. When the primroses appeared, I noticed that the snowdrops weren't so thick anymore. Their stems became limp as soon as I cut them.

When the primroses bloomed, my spirits soared. Their blue, yellow, pink and violet corollas, which would drive a painter mad, stood out on the still wintery ground. A week later, they were hanging dry, not far from the daffodils and irises that were opening in near real time.

No doubt about it. For the first year, the shadow of old age has me feeling death in the midst of the irruption of life. But it's not for lack of warning. Poets, troubadours and storytellers of all countries and times have sung of new flowers as the harbinger of the grave.

"Mignonne, let's go see if the rose…" I recited Ronsard's poem as a child, standing on the stage, like thousands of kids. No doubt I wrote in my reading commentary that "the withered rose evokes for the poet the death of his beloved". I certainly wasn't thinking of *my own* death.

Now I understand why, to my great disappointment, my grandmother used to throw away the bouquets of wild flowers I gave her "because they make a mess with those petals that don't hold". I can hear Aunt Justine's voice: "I prefer artificial flowers because you don't have to change the stinking water." I don't like changing the water either. It reminds me of the cemetery at All Saints' Day, when I was a kid and the adults would send me to empty the Nescafé cans that served as vases, to fill them at the fountain. I'd sniff the rotting water with revulsion. "A corpse must smell like that," I said to myself, with a shudder of disgust.

We who were born after the war, what do we know of the smell of death? Only those who have done their military service or enlisted, those who have lived through conflicts and disasters, know the intolerable smell of decomposed, burnt, tortured flesh.

But I lied to you. I know that smell. A very similar one, anyway. It was when my father, a veterinarian, took me to the slaughterhouse for meat inspection. Ah, those blood-filled aisles, those gutted animals hanging from fangs, and that stench...

Now, this year, I remember those visits to the hangars of death. How old was I? Ten, eleven? The sight of wilted flowers and tarnished water awakened this memory in my delicate old lady nostrils.

Let's stop this self-indulgent melancholy. Let's be positive for once. Yes, death is part of life, present from birth. So, what the hell, let me indulge in the pleasure of flowers, vases and bouquets, since I'm alive.

Chapter XXX
Little Wilted Flower

It's a song from Reunion Island, when it was called Île Bourbon.

Little wilted flower
Beloved little flower...

Yes, at 60, the rose has faded. No need to pretend. When it comes to beauty, all I have to do is remain attractive and not grow too much hair on my chin. I let the wrinkles come, simply nourishing my skin so that it's not too parchment-like.

To carry out this program, I go to a hammam in my neighborhood, on Women's Day, to languish in green pools, get massaged on blue ceramic tiles and drink tea on a silky mattress.

Every month, I go to the beautician. The booth is small and white-polished. Good-natured simplicity. The owner entrusts me to one of her "charming little employees". Samantha (or Rachida) scrutinizes my skin with an expert eye and suggests a treatment for "mature skin" that is "revitalizing", "moisturizing" and "smoothing" with a "lifting effect due to fruit acids". It's understood that I have no other choice. Grapefruit it is!

Mature makes me think of *blackberry* and *plum*. This adjective conjures up images of the dark red plums that grew at the bottom of my great-grandmother's garden. The plum tree's branches leaned over the manure heap, so that the fruit that didn't end up in my grandmother's basket fell onto the heap, where it gently rotted.

The association of ideas disturbs me, because even if I look at myself objectively in the mirror, I don't look like a heeled fruit. One day, when I was betting that this word had been invented by a sadistic communicator, I was contradicted by my *Petit Larousse*:

Mature, feminine noun; 1 - Arrived at maturity; Spécialt: arrived at a certain psychological maturity. 2 - Said of fish ready to spawn.

Still, multinational beauty companies could have taken the trouble to translate the English word *mature.* Would L'Oréal find it too expensive to hire a good translator? Or does this Anglicism have a metalanguage function? Let's not forget that advertising is a science.

These products are very pleasant. The cream smells like baby's milk, with a hint of citrus. The girls' nimble little hands tenderly spread the products, energetically massage, tactfully cleanse, painlessly expel blackheads, gently wipe, pat and knead. These young ladies, almost like children, tell me about their unfinished youths, their boyfriends, their vacations, their weddings, sometimes their babies.

These young women are exquisite with their rosy complexions. Just looking at them makes me feel younger.

Chapter XXXI
Mythical Meetic

Suzanne's voice on the phone is quivering. "I spent the weekend surfing Meetic. I've got a date on Thursday. A really nice guy, you can feel these things, it's like waves that..."

Waves, you bet! We sometimes have the illusion that our libido is calming down, but the flashbacks are merciless. Suddenly, we need to see an erect sex, right there, right now, in close-up, pumped up, ready to satisfy us to the hilt. That's what must have happened to my friend.

When you think about it, the Internet saves us from a lot of folly: going out with rimmel and tight dresses, too much heady perfume, immoderate drinking, shaking things up in a disco, all to end up in an embrace that our drunkenness will have made us forget the next morning.

You're right, Suzanne. Meetic is discreet, efficient and allows us to get to know each other while keeping a cool head, and what's more, while sitting in our excellent armchair in our cosy pyjamas and wool socks.

The best thing to do is to leave it at that and conclude the (*chat*) conversation with a remote masturbation. But alas!

We've remained true to our roots. If our interlocutor likes opera, like us, skiing, like us, Marguerite Duras, like us, making love in the kitchen, like us, eating acras, like us, the meeting becomes inevitable.

I would have liked to advise Suzanne, so happy to have landed an appointment. I've got so much to say! It's all very delicate. All the more so when, inwardly, I wonder about this relentless drive to find a partner and "maintain a sex life". I'm not against sex at 60, but only if you want it. Of course, these digressions were out of place in my telephone conversation.

So I've limited myself to the essentials.

- Are you sure he's divorced?

- For twenty years!" she replies, triumphant.

If she only knew!

I remember this meeting with a professor of philosophy at the Sorbonne, a specialist in Spinoza. It was about three years ago. On the terrace of a café opposite the Luxembourg, I saw an ugly man in a grey suit, whose old cracked leather satchel betrayed his academic credentials. This is the man.

The conversation had been going on for a few minutes, when he dared: "You strike me as a woman who's very sure of her seductive powers."

I'm flabbergasted, because I'm telling you that after a few years of a happy marriage, I never got over my breakup.

I know, of course, that my big roploplos (95 C) induce this kind of remark. Translation: "Say, bimbo, you're not young, but you've got some nice leftovers. There's no denying it, old girl, you're fuckable."

I ignore the allusion. For want of anything better to do, I divert the subject to Spinoza. A fatal error, which earns me a college lecture to die for. I take advantage of a breath in the speaker's galimatias to ask him the cause of his divorce. The professor suddenly loses his academic posture. He takes on a penetrating air, removes his glasses, rests his elbows on the table, brings his face close to mine, looks me straight in the eye:

- I'll be frank.

And what had to be confessed was confessed.

- Actually, I'm not divorced. My wife wouldn't stand for it. But it's a purely formal union (a philosophical formalism, needless to say). She lives in our villa in Finistère. I live in our apartment on rue des Écoles. I only visit her a few days a year. Little free time... Conferences, colloquia, seminars, the whole shebang, planes, invitations... Yada yada yada.

As I've heard this speech before, with a few variations, I finish tasting my dark chocolate ice cream, then plant two kisses on the professor's cheeks and leave him hanging, without asking to share the bill. Don't overdo it.

Ladies in search of love, you can't imagine the number of gardeners growing their roses in the country house to whom "you can't do that".

- This what?

- Divorce...

- They did it to me.

A delicate moment. The suitor searches for words, stammers, concentrates and ends up triumphantly uttering the word "*gratitude*", in nine cases out of ten. These gentlemen are "indebted" to Bobonne for having wiped the kids, kept the house running and tolerated their misdemeanors. They can do no less than express their *gratitude*, a talismanic word for cowards. All the more so since their wife, who has been laid to rest in cellophane, will be reactivated as a nurse in old age.

Let's not gossip. I have two friends in their sixties who found their mate on the Internet. They must have something. I suspect they put "Catholic" in the "religion" question. Or "Protestant". Protestant's safer, isn't it?

Chapter XXXII
Dogs Soften the Blow

Five of us in our sixties are out walking our dogs in the afternoon. The conversation, initially devoted to the dogs, gradually moves on to more varied subjects. A friendship takes shape.

To move in this direction, we need strategic information.

Marie is the first to cast her probing spell. While we're talking cinema, she says:

- I find Woody Allen too intellectual, except in his latest films. Alain, on the other hand, is a real fan.

"Alain" is the marker emitted by the walker to signal that she has a husband named Alain. Received loud and clear by Justine, who wags her tail (er, I mean, shakes her head).

- Well, we're the opposite! I'm an unconditional fan, while Henri is always in a foul mood when it comes to his films. So we go to the same cinema to see two different films.

- That's the contract I signed with Jean-Luc," adds Geneviève.

An angel passes. Christine stands motionless. I dare myself.

- In art, to each his own. It's like our adorable dogs. Some prefer Fido, others Canaillou.

Missed. Our little committee now consists of two groups. Three married women and two single women. This polarization puts electricity in the air. The wives are on the verge of yelping that it's well done, no doubt we wanted to play the free woman. Result: we drink the bitter cup of solitude.

Wives, aren't you tired of taking care of your gouty patients? After being cuckolded all your lives, maybe!

Our dogs, sniffing out the ambient tension, begin to turn, to growl and to growl. The storm is approaching. We walk silently into the heavy sky.

Can you believe it? The wind shifts suddenly. Something warns us to avoid a fight.

What happened? I tell myself the Penelope tenacity is old-fashioned, but not lacking in panache. I don't know what's going through her head, but Christine, my goodness, looks serene. And the wives? They may think that with an hour's walk a day, Christine and I have little chance of seducing their husbands. Do they think we have our little habits as single women? Who can blame us for meeting a discreet lover?

I conjecture, but the result is there: like old canines who disdain provocation, we tacitly decide to forgo the little game of perfidious insinuations. Aren't we five older women who have sailed here and there in search of a precarious balance between love and passion, adventure and routine?

We set off again at a leisurely pace through the park, chatting like real girlfriends with our pooches on our heels.

Chapter XXXIII
Sleeping in

I open my eyes around eight in the morning. I listen voluptuously to the cavalcade of schoolchildren beneath my window. Three blocks away, the "click-clack" of shoes, hurrying not to miss the train, approaches the house, then decreases.

I go down to the kitchen for breakfast and quickly slip back between the sheets.

Strollers squeaking, babies crying, laughter, garbage cans rumbling. The morning begins.

Staying at the bottom of the bed listening to the neighborhood on the alert, in a hurry, growling, scraping, is a music more suave than the most exquisite symphony.

Tucked up against the pillows, I read. I bathe in words. I perfume myself in the foam of words. At intervals, I open a notebook and scribble. Writing projects, an unknown term, the trace of a dream, the profile of a character I might bring to life. For whole minutes, I forget about reading and the notebook. I think of nothing. I look at nothing. Empty moments. My white curtains filter the light.

No need to make an early phone call. People are in "transport", perched on cafeteria stools, in elevators, in toilets, in office corridors. When I think they've *roughly* read their e-mails and got down to work, I put the book down. The trick is to catch them before "the meeting". There's only one way: telepathy. It works pretty well. I've got a lot of experience!

My bed turns into a lazy man's "office". Mac, telephone, books, papers, Post-its, newspapers on the comforter, I'm "working". That's putting it mildly... A few relics of my former profession, preserved by superstition, appointments to note down, e-mail chats. Nonchalantly. No need to rush.

"You won't age well if you stay in bed!" My conscience never reproaches me for this. After so many years of forcing myself to get up early: to revise lessons, to cram for competitions, to drop the kids off at school, to go to the office, to finish a report, to wrap up an article, I feel in my right mind. Almost half a century! That's enough. My late mornings are a daily delight. It's only around noon, a little less, a little more, that I put a toe on the ground.

For a while, I resumed my "disciplined" lifestyle.

With the window open, I give myself a muscular workout, make my bed, wash up and get dressed. Time to walk my dog. I pass a retired neighbor who greets me.

"Hello, how are you Madeleine, in shape? Me, I'm dead tired! I've vacuumed the carpets, done two loads of washing and drained my ironing pile. I've got one of those lumbar pains! I'm off to the physio, you know the one who replaced the... blah, blah, blah."

What a killjoy, that one! If I'd known, I'd have stayed an extra hour under the comforter, just to get away from her early-bird chatter. Or her lies, who knows?

Chapter XXXIV
My Sherpas

My children, aged 26 and 31, have offered to take me for a walk. It's nice of them to come and stroll along a country lane for my pleasure, rather than indulge in some more athletic climbing.

"Don't worry, I know the route," I said. "I've got my bearings. After the town hall, a steep incline, then a reservoir and a donkey at the stake, and it's straight on."

Behind the town hall, after the steep slope, no more well than donkey. The grass has probably hidden the well. And the donkey? Well, the donkey's dead. How many years does a donkey live? Anyway, there's a path. We're moving on.

Very soon, the path turns into crevassed ground, full of stones. We look down at our feet. Silence. Suddenly, a line of black paint on a stone jumps out at me. Like a satanic sign, the black paint marks paths "for very experienced walkers".

I took a completely wrong route.

My kids laugh under their breath. A black girl! This is going to be great. At the same time, they realize that their sexagenarian mother is in for a rough ride. Tactfully, my son moves to the front and my daughter to the back.

Two dashing thoroughbred horses and an elderly donkey — that's what our caravan is all about.

We approach an area lined with flat, sharp stones that slide underfoot like snakes, while a terrifying cliff looms ahead. My dilapidated hip (this was before my prosthesis was fitted) throws lightning shocks at me. I stare at my son's shoes to keep going.

Inflexible, the sun rises. My socks are soaked, the sweat slides down my back, soaking my underwear. The ordeal lasts two hours. Then the stones disappear. The path twists and turns. The forest becomes thick. There are a few shady spots. Only then do the young men give me a break. They serve me water, but only a little. "Drinking too much makes you thirsty." "Don't sit down, it cuts your legs." I lean against a tree trunk. Ten minutes and off we go again!

An hour later, we come out onto a devilishly windy mountain pasture. From here, we dominate the cliffs. Below, a heat haze freezes the landscape, which stretches beyond the Rhône, shining like glass, and opens out on the other side onto the Vercors mountains. The wind, the perspective, the altitude, intoxicate me. I sink into the grass.

"Picnic", announced my sherpas. But there's no way I'm going to eat what I've prepared! From my generous cold meal, the young men extract three Vache qui rit, three slices of bread and three cookies. We need to eat light to tackle the descent. I beg for a nap. They concede: "Ten minutes, no more." Just long enough to sniff the grass, gaze at two grasshoppers, chew a strand of oats, and the gong rings.

We start the descent. In the hairpin bends, I try my hand at trotting. Woouf, I slip. Craaac, I rip my Bermuda shorts all the way down the back seam, triggering a triple giggle.

Back at the scree, the fun's over. I'm scared. Yes, afraid of slipping, of twisting my foot, of cutting myself on the way down. I shout "ouch", "ouch", "ouh là là" and "wait for me! I crab forward in my split Bermuda shorts. Sad posture!

When we return to the crevassed passageway, I beg my children to go ahead and pick me up in their car. "No way!" they retort. "If you've made it this far, one more kilometer isn't going to kill you."

They spared me the humiliation of abandoning the race. Reinvigorated, when it's time to get back in the car, I make a point of getting behind the wheel.

What fulfillment! What a victory! An inner voice whispers to me: "This may be the last time I ever hike like this." I don't grieve at the thought.

Chapter XXXV
A Weekend in Brittany

Saint-Brieuc. On the blue station sign, I read this name playing the biniou. Pchuuuu... The TGV door slides open. I'm embraced by the soft, iodized, humid air. I rent a car and head for Paimpol. Hedged fields, low houses, gorse... Suddenly, the cliff and the sea. Only three kilometers to go.

Here are the white gates, the hydrangeas, the granite walls, the small windows. Bernard is my eldest, but we hardly notice the difference. For him, 1939. For me, 1945. The war separates us. Everywhere, in life, we carried our six-year age gap. The same elementary school in Montélimar, the same lycée, the same studies in Lyon, the same "ascent to Paris", the same profession. Our families knew each other well. His friends had little brothers and sisters my age.

Bernard is a merry man and an outraged one at that. He's an ecological anarchist, a purist, a polemicist, a pamphleteer. I was a dedicated activist, then a serious journalist. We couldn't be more different. And yet, there's something fraternal between us, no doubt because of our successive lives. I love coming to his place. We talk, we read, we listen to jazz, we argue. Friends drop in. We laugh, we belittle, we drink. We eat, we kiss, we yell at each

other: "old anarchist", "Trotskyite bastard", "indecent Stalinist"...
It's a party!

When I turn off my engine on March 8, 2012, he comes to the gate. He smiles broadly into his gray beard. He's wearing his eternal velvet pants. Over them, I notice a robe. He's lost weight. He says to me:

"Come on in, would you like something to drink?"

He brings out the calva. He continues with the list of festivities:

"Marie-Ange will be coming to dinner with Paulo and Marc, do you know Marc? Petit Jean will be there too, but I'm not sure, well, we'll see."

As usual, we'll see.

"So, if you want a drink, help yourself, because I only drink wine now. Well, it's not allowed, but I do. (*Laughs.*) Bring your suitcase inside. And your dog, is your dog here?"

Of course he's here, my dog, already sniffing out Bernard's dogs, circling around them and them in turn.

Bernard's big voice:

"Brel, Gainsbourg, here!"

The order is lost in a rattle. The robe parted. He's so emaciated that his pants fall to his hips. I see the pocket.

"Damn pocket!" he exclaims. The nurse is coming to change it later."

He looks exhausted. I let the dogs out.

So, Bernard, how are you getting on with the chemo?

Well, more or less. They found metastases in my liver. They think it's in my bones. But it's not certain. We'll have to wait for the X-rays. Here, can you give me my glasses? (He grabs the *Brest Telegram*.) Read this! "Our senior team wins the Côtes-d'Armor Cup". See, it's dated five months ago. Just after your last visit.

Imagine, I won the senior tennis cup, I was in top form. No warning signs. I had taken a hemocult test and it was negative. Ne-ga-tive! I understood when I bled. They operated on my ass, the most homophobic of French journalists. Wrong. They operated on me a second time, then took an X-ray, then did that damn chemo.

- Come on, this bone thing, it's not safe. They just want to check it out. Because of lawsuits and stuff. Over 50% of cancers are cured today.

- You sound like my brother, the doctor. He predicts: "You'll be fine." An excellent practitioner, my brother.

(*Smiles.*) It's those hospital sessions that wear me out.

He shows me his morphine pump.

- It's a good thing I have this.

The door shakes. Friends arrive. We open the bottles. We drink. We laugh. We shout. We call each other names. We have fun. The women cook. The usual.

At midnight, the audience is drunk on words and wine. Bernard has dozed off in his armchair. He snores, as always.

The next morning, when I get up, he's still sitting. I let the dogs out. I come back in. I go to the kitchen to make coffee.

He opens one eye.

- Not too strong, the coffee!

- Yes, I know, I know. Did you stay in the chair all night?

- No! I went to bed, but I can't sleep. It hurts too much. So I put myself here. Then I went back to bed. At last, I'm commuting.

He presses the remote control. Soccer. The usual. Hours of soccer. But Bernard doesn't watch.

He's dozing.

Suddenly, I hear him screaming because Manchester United have scored. He shouts "Well done!", stuffing his pipe. I go to get the coffee. When I come back with the tray, he's asleep. His head has rolled forward and the pipe has fallen on the tiles.

I left on March 12. He told me, with his good laugh:

"Be careful on the road."

As usual. On May 23, he passed away.

Montélimar cemetery:

"It was too hard. It was better for him to go."

As an aside, the well-meaning, who came to his funeral because he came from an honorable family, murmured:

"With the life he led…"

Yes, as soon as he's in the hole, he's saying it's all his fault. He drank too much, smoked too much, fucked too much. Words like *lust* and *fornication* no longer apply. They've become medicalized. In the logic of aging well, we'll talk about poor lifestyle hygiene.

One who has lived a healthy life is Agnès. Agnès is a miracle worker. Not of her cancer, which she died of at just 60. From her ruptured aneurysm. At 25, pregnant, just like that, on an ordinary day, in the kitchen. Coma. They don't pull the plug, because the fetus lives on. The child, a boy, was born by Caesarean section. The family, very religious, forbade the young woman's life to be terminated after the birth of her son. A miracle of faith: after two years, Agnès-Belle came to her senses. Few after-effects. Slight muscle atony on the right, voice a little hoarse from the tracheotomy.

Agnès is a graphic designer and press cartoonist. She resumed her work. She paints, she exhibits. And then, at 58, *boom*, cancer. First breast, as is often the case, then elsewhere.

Agnès is having chemo. She says with a smile that it's convenient because the oncology center is on her metro line. Agnès has lost weight and hair. With her hats and loose-fitting clothes, she's a real looker. Agnès has class.

For Christmas, since she knows I'm alone, she invites me. Her son, her son's partner, a few journalist friends. Foie gras, coq au riesling, champagne. For each, a drawing in her hand. Two months later, I phone. No one's there. I call her son. She had to go to hospital, in palliative care. Two months, no more. Her ashes were scattered in the carré des anonymes at Père-Lachaise, according to her wishes.

Personal stories? Yes, very. Don't forget, as you read them, that Agnès and Bernard are among the 33% of "premature deaths" that take place before the age of 60. Those who develop cancer after that age are supernumeraries in the statistics. Curious expression, isn't it, "cancer declares itself"? It's like an actor stepping to the front of the stage to proclaim: "I declare the festival open."

For the moment, I've escaped the declarative announcement. The same goes for my cousin Marine, the nurse. Her breast cancer has been cured. Proof that the figures are right. Two out of three breast cancers end in a *happy ending*. Marine has "triumphed" over her cancer, as the headlines say, after a "battle" in which her "morale" played a "major role". It's a hell of a job fighting cancer, a full-time job. So Marine took a sick leave. When she was almost cured, but still had to watch out for a possible recurrence, she went back to work part-time. Everyone was happy, Marine, her colleagues and her bosses at the hospital. Well done, Marine! When her recovery was complete, she asked for full-time work. It's not easy living on half pay. The bosses:

"So close to retirement? Why don't you take early retirement? It would be wiser, as you're likely to overwork yourself."

And to insist. A lot. Marine stood her ground. The law had to be applied.

That's when the mood changed. Full-time, my 59-year-old cousin, weakened by the battle against her cured cancer, wasn't productive enough. Colleagues:

"Your courage, certainly, commands admiration, but in the meantime, we're stuffing ourselves with work for you."

Now you understand why my cousin didn't pot.

But time goes by and I still don't have cancer. The more the years go by, the less risk I run, since most cancers start before the age of 60 and decrease thereafter. When I'm 100, the risk will be close to zero. Why am I bickering and nitpicking? It's good news, isn't it?

Chapter XXXVI
Turn the Rides Around!

Ah, funfairs, their glitz, their bad taste, the male voices in the crackling microphones, the churros, the neon strips, the dusty floor, the discordant music, the cotton candy...

These parties are for young people: they've got to shine, they've got to flash, they've got to blow your mind.

"Come on, youth, come on, there's only two minutes left for the big jump, the big thrill, the complete 360° tour! Get on board, young people, come on, miss, get on, come on, don't hesitate! You want thrills? You want speed? Then take your place on the super roller coaster, triple loop, forward and reverse rotation, the only one of its kind in Europe, for just five euros!"

I hand over five euros, take a ticket, sit down in a row of four, take off my glasses.

Neighbors snicker:

"Grandma, you better get down here before it starts! You're going to give us a stroke, Granny."

Young people elbow each other in front and behind. They turn, giggle. I hear:

"No, but I'm hallucinating, did you see that? Does she want to kill herself, or what?"

A rascal lowers the steel hoops that lock me to the back of the chair. Impossible to retract! No more yelling: "Alert, I want to get off! Irreversibility fuels the pleasure.

The merry-go-round starts up. It moves so slowly that I feel as if I'm falling asleep. I watch the square slide by in slow motion, see the other rides go by, look up. The trees turn without hurrying, the sky becomes rounder.

I let myself be lulled by the gentle roll. Ah, if only death could be received this way! I detect a slight acceleration, the square turns faster, the colors merge. A jolt warns me that we've left the platform, I climb, I climb, I brush against the leaves of the plane trees, I see the square below. No sooner have I taken this cue than I'm jolted, swaying back and forth, left and right. From the depths comes the muffled voice of the man with the microphone.

"So, how's youth?" From all sides, we shout, I shout "OUIIIIIIIIIII!"

"You want more? - YES!"

Young people close their eyes, Valkyries shout war cries.

"Careful!" says the cavernous voice, "now we're going full circle. Are you ready, youth? - YES!"

Let's get rolling! Each row begins to roll in on itself. Screaming, pitching and rolling, my head sinks, I catch a glimpse of the indistinct crowd, I can't stand it any longer, I'm going to close my eyes... But already the movement is slowing down. Faces return to their places. I breathe in.

The man at the microphone asks in a teasing voice:

"You want more? You want more?"

Un "OUIIIIIIIIIIIIIIIIII" se propage, le micro enchaîne.

"So, let's do it again, one more little trip to the stars, let's go!"

Everything speeds up, everything melts away again, the second lap seems tedious, I close my eyes and wait for it to slow down. Phew! The mechanism weakens, the jolts diminish, then the ride comes to a halt, even though it seems to me that my body is still flying. The big rascal releases me from my hoops. The youngsters stand up, dazed, unbalanced, embracing, laughing and proud. My legs feel like absorbent cotton. I wobble towards the exit staircase.

Audiences look at me like I'm an alien. They're right. I've come back from another planet. The day I don't feel like taking a ride anymore, I'll be really old.

CONCLUSION
BEFORE THE END...

As you may have guessed, I'm not going to give you my five precepts or my ten rules for living.

Don't think I'm suffering from an obsessive fixation on certain authors, HR consultants retrained in humanitude.

What irritates me is that their accounting, apart from showing a certain narrow-mindedness and offering advice that's laughably silly, is —precisely— accounting, i.e. a way of managing human resources that calibrates everything, measures everything, puts everything through the performance mill.

Our coaches teach us nothing more and nothing less than how to "manage our ageing capital". The French National Plan for Ageing Well speaks of "intellectual, physical, social and psychological capital". This is for the global, which can be infinitely subdivided into as many (market) segments. A brand of dairy desserts urges us to preserve our "bone capital". The same applies to heart, liver, veins, blood, muscles, neurology and so on, *ad infinitum.*

The lexical fields of value and savings are used in all their forms. One of our coaches, Isabelle le Bouëtté, defines her doctrine as follows: "Living better with ourselves allows us to age in better health and to provide others with the added value that corresponds to us." *Bien-être et Santé* magazine, available free in pharmacies, follows suit: "Adopting a lifestyle that's good for the body after 50 and even 70 [delicious, that "even"...] is still profitable."

Of course, as a journalist, I know that my colleagues and others who want to clarify their statements are rightly looking for comparisons to avoid boilerplate terms and repetition. We can't always use the adjectives *beneficent, good* or *wise*. Except that, as the CAIRN magazine (which brings together various humanities publications under its banner) points out in its 2003 issue: "Words are not neutral. They translate and construct social processes."

Many sociologists, even after Marx and Engels went out of fashion, have written books arguing that old age is a social construct. This is borne out by the ambivalence of this stage of life in many civilizations, and even within them. The "old man", who begins at various ages —including our own— is sometimes the wise man consulted by the community, the venerable old man, even a white-bearded deity (or the one and only God), sometimes a withered, frail, impure and smelly form.

In Greek mythology, old age was sent to men by Zeus to punish them for having opened Pandora's box, basically for not having been able to resist giving in to curiosity.

In Russian, *starik* means old man in general (rather neutral), *starets* respectable old man, *staritchok* decrepit old man. Examples are legion and sometimes comical. In *Oedipus at Colonus*, Sophocles laments old age, even though he wrote the tragedy at the age of 88!

Anthropologists, for their part, have published monographs on societies where old age as a distinct phase of life does not exist.

The Cuevas Indians of Colombia, for example, distinguish only three categories: men, women and children. In this nomadic Amerindian population, the elderly participate to the best of their ability in communal life, without any separation from the young, whether men or women.

A fine argument for abolishing all pension schemes, wouldn't you say? Of course, it would be backward-looking to assign us to basket-weaving, in the name of some rural or clan-based society (the last expressions of which modern capitalism hunts down so as not to stand in the way of the free circulation of goods in the global world). But isn't selling MacDonald's at a drive-in, while sitting on a stool in a gatehouse, about to become furiously trendy?

Lessons from the past are a delicate matter. They should, however, lead us to avoid the schizophrenic postmodern discourse which, as you may know, foresees only two outcomes to our civilizational crisis. I'm talking here about the developed countries, because elsewhere —globalization or not— the majority of human beings have other urgent concerns (let's add that, despite general alienation, there are some earthlings, even in inner-city Paris, whom the harshness of daily life prompts to think of something else).

The first approach postulates that, at around 60, the approximate age of retirement, there is a "caesura" that allows us to start all over again, a "new age" during which we, the young, hand-some, wealthy and fit seniors, will rebuild our lives, our culture, our loves, reshape our desires and make our dreams come true, with minor health inconveniences considered minor and very easy to overcome (and the question of old age "settled" thanks to long-term care insurance coupled with funeral insurance).

The second perspective is radically catastrophic. It concedes that we are beautiful, rich… but that this state of affairs is highly precarious. Historically, we will be the last generation to "enjoy" "good pensions". Our children will become impoverished and downgraded. They'll have to work much longer than we do, and may never receive a pension. They'll be gray-haired bums. All we can do is limit the damage by not burdening them (long-term care and funeral insurance, as in hypothesis 1) and by helping them (family mutual aid, donations).

That history is non-linear, that it experiences ruptures or that mankind is capable of inventing new solutions are hypotheses to be classified as utopias and lost illusions. Since the fall of the Wall, this has been as irrefragable a certainty as the hardest metamorphic rock. An event that happened a quarter of a century ago…

Precarious, for us too. We're told: OK, so far so good, you're retired, in good shape, etc. But beware! But watch out! (*Here, coaches and consultants enter the scene*). You have to preserve this capital and manage it skilfully. Which means: daily walks, weekly shagging, no more cigarettes, a glass of wine a day (for the heart and the union of winegrowers), world travel and sex tourism if you like, club life, crosswords and everything else I've described to you in abundance.

The key word in this final chapter is pre-sale! Don't forget to "invest" in the single-storey home, in the bathroom with its opening bathtub and invigorating water jets, in the seals to put under the Persian rugs, in the stairlift that looks like a toilet in a washroom (I give these details, (I'm giving you these details because I'm afraid I haven't devoted a chapter, however well-deserved, to equipping the home of the sexagenarian), not to mention the earth-scraping devices in the garden that prevent you from having to bend down, and a thousand inventions from the Lépine competition for the use of sexas.

If you've skipped the preceding paragraphs, finding them a tad repetitive, that's okay, because you can see where I'm going with this.

As Michel Billé and Didier Martz put it in their excellent book *La Tyrannie du bien vieillir (The Tyranny of Ageing Well)*: "If ageing well becomes a personal and political project from which no one can derogate, ageing badly becomes a mistake, almost a crime, both for oneself and for those who will have to bear the consequences [...] This apparently innocuous expression then takes on the status of an 'idol' in the Nietzschean sense of the term. If we're not careful, it insinuates itself into our consciousness by breaking in.

But what do you do, you ask, and quite rightly so, when your three children and ten grandchildren arrive at your country house and the pool has just turned green from the heat?

I answer. Do nothing. Are you disappointed? I understand. In this case, let them figure it out. Or give them the phone number of the pool man you're paying with your rich daddy's retirement home money.

On a more serious note, disregard the advice you're given. At the very most, skim through our coaches' columns in magazines and journals and skim to retain, if need be, the frail film that will be useful to you.

By doing nothing, I also mean imposing nothing on you that would be dictated in the name of the new life you would be granted. You don't erase the blackboard to write a new text at 60. Of course, the transition to retirement induces a caesura.

Another stage awaits us around this anniversary, even though we're persuaded that it doesn't, so that we have to admit that everything is starting again, but that we haven't changed.

To do nothing is also to live without "doing", and therefore without "acting". We're lucky enough to escape action, the meaning of salaried work, performance and other objective contracts. Let's make the most of it! Let's not get bogged down with a twelve-step "life project"! On the contrary, let's let laziness take over, good laziness, fruitful inactivity. Let's sleep in or get up early, go to bed with the chickens or with the night owls... or... you get the idea.

There's no need to feel guilty about this inaction and laziness. We don't have to feel "guilty" about our descendants (if we have any). Our sons and daughters had their childhoods marked by the tribulations of the '68 generation. Ours, by that of our parents, sons of the War and the Trente Glorieuses who stood up, like the statue of the Commander, to tell us that their heroism was unique.

Let's take a step back. Let's look at the young people of this planet, the young Tunisians, Afghans, Turks, Palestinians, Syrians... Let's look at those of our own time, in Chile, Argentina, the former USSR, who lost their lives or their minds for causes that we condescendingly say were lost in advance, if not suspect. Let's look at those in their 40s and 50s, the Croats, Serbs and Kosovars who lived through childhood and adolescence during the last Balkan conflict, all these strata of a thin peel of recent history, and stop whining about our kids!

They will invent their future; they are already inventing their present. We don't have to build our sixties in relation to our children, it's the world upside down.

What then? Nothing else. Just this beautiful quote gleaned for you while writing this book: "To live is to grow old and to grow old is to live." But maybe?

Maybe tomorrow I'll climb up a stepladder to get some jam and break my right hip, and since I already have a prosthesis on my left, I'll have a sloping surface built between the kitchen and the dining room, which will cost me so much that I'll take out long-term care insurance for the rest of the work?

Maybe this winter I'll get dressed up to go to the theater and find myself looking so pale and my skin so cracked that the very next day I'll book an appointment at a beauty clinic for a full assessment of what's left of my beauty capital?

Perhaps, having opened the invitation (print) following the announcement (web) of the Parti Socialiste and Associates popular ball at the 19th arrondissement town hall, I drank two glasses of scotch, put on a miniskirt and drunkenly stuck to a dancer of some 70 years of age, of North African type, still green?

I'm a frail, thinking reed...

And yet, dear readers, this admission of weakness is not an expression of cultural relativism or a concession to the "free-for-all" or "enjoy unfettered".

No. I pride myself on having a "backbone", principles and convictions. I don't believe that everything equals everything, nor that all opinions are equal, but I am aware of my limits. I simply wish to help you consider, or rather consider with you, how we sexagenarians might remain free, as we wished (or thought) to be at 20. As I would like to leave this life, and as I wish for you.

BIBLIOGRAPHY

Books

ALLARD (Michel), *Le Grand Défi: tous centenaires et en bonne santé*, Paris, Olivier Orban, 1991.

BADOU (Gérard), *Les Nouveaux Vieux*, Paris, Le Pré aux clercs, 1985.

BEAUVOIR (Simone de), *La Vieillesse*, Paris, Gallimard, "collections Idées", volumes I and II, 1985.

BILLÉ (Michel), *La Chance de vieillir*, essai de gérontologie sociale, Paris, L'Harmattan, 2004.

BILLÉ (Michel) and MARTZ (Didier), *La Tyrannie du Bien vieillir*, Lormont, Le Bord de l'Eau Éditions, 2010.

BONVALET (Catherine) and OGG (Jim), *Les Baby-boomers : une génération mobile*, La Tour-d'Aigues, éditions INED/L'Aube, 2009.

BOURDELAIS (Patrice), *L'Âge de la vieillesse, histoire du vieillissement de la population*, Paris, Odile Jacob, 1993.

BOIS (Jean-Pierre), *Les Vieux: de Montaigne aux premières retraites*, Paris, Fayard, 1989.

CICERO, *De senectute*, Paris, Éditions Arlea, 1990.

DERKENNE (Françoise), *Le Temps de la bienvieillance*, Médialogues, 1987.

DUBOIS-DUMÉE (Jean-Pierre), *Vieillir sans devenir vieux*, Paris, Desclée de Brouwer, 1991.

DYTCHWALD (Ken) and CICUREL (Michel), *Age Wave*, Los Angeles, Jeremy P. Tarcher, 1989.

FRANCK (Michel), *Planète sexe, tourismes sexuels, marchandisation et déshumanisation des corps*, Paris, Homnisphères, 2006. - *Voyage au bout du sexe, trafics et tourismes sexuels en Asie et ailleurs*, Laval, Presses de l'université de Laval (Québec), 2007.

GÉNÉREUX (Jacques), *La Dissociété*, Paris, Éditions du Seuil, 2006.

GUITTON (Jean-Pierre), *Naissance du vieillard. Essai sur l'histoire des rapports entre les vieillards et la société en France*, Paris, Aubier, 1988.

GOSSARD (Renate) and HUGUENIN (Jacques), *La Révolte des vieilles*, Paris, L'Harmattan, 2003.

LEVET (Maximilienne) and PELLETIER (Chantal), *Papy Boom*, Paris, Grasset, 1988.

MINOIS (Georges), *Histoire de la vieillesse de l'Antiquité à la Renaissance*, Lyon, Decitre, 1994.

MUFFANG (Sophie), *La Retraite? Pas si simple! Comment passer le cap*, Paris, Ellipses, 2010.

PUIJALON (Bernadette) and trinCAz (Jacqueline), *Le Droit de vieillir*, Paris, Fayard, 2000.

PASCAL (Blaise), *Pensées*, Paris, Gallimard, 2004.

RIGAUD (Jacques), *Le Bénéfice de l'âge*, Paris, Grasset, 1994.

RIVIÈRE (Carole-Anne) and BRUGIÈRE (Amandine), *Bien vieillir grâce au numérique*, Limoges, FYP Éditions, 2010.

SANSOT (Pierre), *Du bon usage de la lenteur*, Paris, Payot, 1988.

SÉNÈQUE, *De la brièveté de la vie*, Paris, Garnier-Flammarion, 2005.

Schuster-Cordone (Caroline), *Le Crépuscule des corps. Images de la vieillesse féminine*, Fribourg, In-Folio, 2009.

Treguer (Jean-Paul), *Le Senior marketing*, Paris, Dunod, 1994.

Vinot (Pierre), *Déjà la retraite et je ne suis même pas prêt(e)! Petit traité pour réussir sa retraite*, Brussels, André Versaille Éditions, 2011.

Articles

Arcand (Bernard), *The Cultural Construction of Old Age. Anthropologie et société*, n°3, vol. VI, Quebec City, Department of Anthropology, Laval University, 1982.

Chapuis-Lucciani (Nicole), *L'Anthropologie biologique: une approche holistique pour étudier le vieillissement humain. L'anthropologie du vivant, objets et méthodes*, 2010.

CAIRN Info: "Vieillesse et exclusion sociale", thematic issue of *Pensée Plurielle*, no. 6, Boeck Université, 2003.

"Old age and the love of the world", *Esprit*, n°366, 2010.

Fortunato and Drusini, "Étude sur les vieux dans la tribu Quechua au Pérou", *Journal of Cross-cultural Gerontology*, n°20, 2005.

Gamotti (Dr), "État de santé", GHPS (Groupe histoire, philosophie, sciences), 2006.

Gérontologie et société, n°138, September 2011. Thematic issue on housing for the elderly.

Plan national Bien vieillir 2007-2009, published by the French High Council for Public Health.

"Les relations intergénérationnelles", *Politiques sociales et familiales*, n°105, September 2011.

Vallin and Meslé, "Peut-on gagner trois mois indéfiniment?", *Population et Sociétés*, n°473, December 2010.

SUNIGA, "Gerontology and the sense of time", *Revue internatio-
nale d'action communautaire,* ⁿᵒˢ 23/63.

Sites
agevillage.com
bienvieillir.com
doctissimo.com
generactions.com
passeportsante.com
seniorboulevard.com- senioragency.com
and many more...

Table of Contents

Best sellers Max Milo Editions

Hitler's banker, Jean-François Bouchard

Confessions of a forger, Éric Piedoie Le Tiec

The Koran and the flesh, Ludovic-Mohamed Zahed

Governing by fake news, Jacques Baud

Governing by chaos, Collectif

A political history of food, Paul Ariès

Mad in U.S.A.: The ravages of the "American model",
Michel Desmurget

Mondial soccer club geopolitics, Kévin Veyssière

Putin: Game master?, Jacques Braud

Treatise on the three impostors: Moses, Jesus, Muhammad,
The Spirit of Spinoza

TV Lobotomy, Michel Desmurget